New Hampshire Rail Trails

NEW ENGLAND RAIL HERITAGE SERIES
from Branch Line Press

The Rail Lines of Southern New England
Ronald Dale Karr

Lost Railroads of New England, Second Edition
Ronald Dale Karr

The Rail Lines of Northern New England
Robert M. Lindsell

*A Field Guide to Southern New England Railroad Depots
and Freight Houses*
John H. Roy, Jr.

New Hampshire Rail Trails
Charles F. Martin

New Hampshire Rail Trails

CHARLES F. MARTIN

Branch
Line
Press

PEPPERELL, MASSACHUSETTS

Printed in the United States of America by P. A. Hutchison, Mayfield, PA, on 30% post-consumer recycled paper.

Branch Line Press
30 Elm Street
Pepperell, Massachusetts 01463-1603

Email: books@branchlinepress.com
www.branchlinepress.com

Cover design by Diane B. Karr
Book design by Ronald Dale Karr

Cover photographs by the author, except as noted. Front: Presidential Range Rail Trail, Pondicherry Section; Insert: Detail of 1933 Henniker Jct. photo on page 101; Back, left: Northern Rail Trail in Merrimack County (Peter Southworth); center: Out-of-service track on former Wilton rail line; right: Southeast Region rail trail.

Library of Congress Cataloging-in-Publication Data

Martin, Charles Fontaine, 1945-
  New Hampshire rail trails / Charles F. Martin.
    p. cm. -- (New England rail heritage series)
  Includes bibliographical references and index.
  ISBN 978-0-942147-10-0 (pbk.)
  1. Rail-trails--New Hampshire--Guidebooks. I. Title. II. Series.

GV191.42.N4M326 2008
917.4204'44--dc22

                              2008006748

10   9   8   7   6   5   4   3   2

Rail trails don't just happen. They result from efforts of volunteer groups and support by individuals in local, state, and federal organizations. This book is dedicated to all who have developed and continue to improve New Hampshire rail trails.

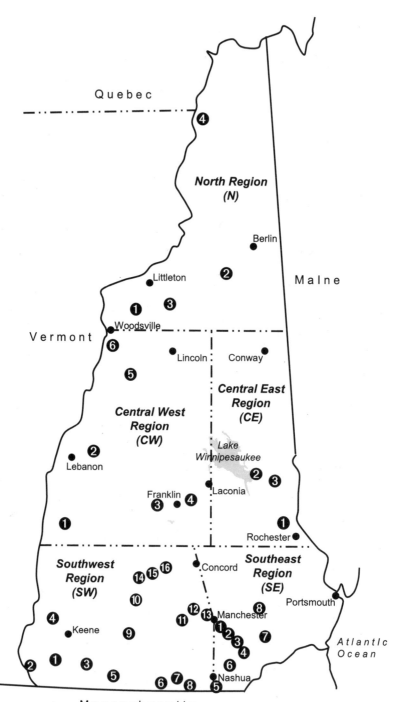

Contents

Southeast Region 125

Central West Region 180

Central East Region 228

North Region 249

Helpful Organizations 291

Additional Resources 295

Index 298

About the Author 304

Addendum to Second Printing

ATV Use Now Prohibited on Many Trails

Just after this book went to print, the Federal Highway Administration ruled that ATVs (All Terrain Vehicles) and motorized trail bikes are not snow machines and hence cannot be used on trails developed with Transportation Enhancement funds. Previously these vehicles had been categorized with snowmobiles and were allowed in winter, when the trails were covered with snow. This ruling prohibits ATV use on the following trails: Cheshire North, Cheshire South, Ashuelot, Fort Hill, Monadnock, Portsmouth Branch, Londonderry, Northern, Farmington, Wolfeboro, and Upper Coos.

Trail Improvements

Many New Hampshire trails have been extended or improved in the two years since the book's first printing. The Northern Rail Trail, for example, is now an improved four-season trail all the way from Lebanon Center to Franklin Center. The Hands Across the Merrimack Bridge was completed and leads to a beautiful, paved, Piscataquog Trail to the Piscataquog Reservoir bridge. Some of the most challenging obstacles for trail users—such as those pictured on pages 66, 82, and 110—have been fixed. In general, the trails are in as good or better shape than described in the book. One notable exception is a giant slide of earth fill on the extension of the South Manchester Trailway described on page 136.

Information Updates

Regrettably, I have not had time to keep up the book's companion web site with information on trail changes. The best resources for current rail trail news are:

- The Bike-Walk Alliance of New Hampshire web site, *http://www.bwanh.org*; click on "NH Rail Trail News."

- The New Hampshire Rail Trails Coalition web site, *http://www.NHRailTrails.org*. This may change to *http://www.NHRTC.org*.

- The New Hampshire Bureau of Trails web site, *http://www.nhstateparks.org/explore/bureau-of-trails/*

CHARLES MARTIN

November 2010

Foreword

I HAVE BEEN involved in the world of rail trail advocacy for over twelve years now and have met thousands of people along the way. Many of these people I have met on the trail, but more still at meetings related to trail development. It has always been my goal to get the word out about these places. Getting them noticed more, rediscovered, or discovered in the first place is critical, because a significant number of people who experience them will—like me and Charles—have a life-changing moment. A moment where they can say with certainty, "The first time I ever walked or jogged or rode my bike on a rail trail, something just clicked in me and I said to myself...*Brilliant!*"

One of the interesting and important things about rail trails is how they slowly yet inexorably change communities. You, too, will discover that the longer a developed trail has been in place, the more oriented the surrounding community becomes toward people-scale activities (as opposed to automobile-scale activities). Downtowns become revitalized and down-home community values are enhanced. These special routes offer residents a way to reconnect people, neighborhoods, and entire towns in a way that has been almost forgotten. These special paths are not just "cute paths in the woods" that meander around nowhere; they lead to village centers, schools, shopping, and services, providing basic connections between places where people live, work, and play.

In a 100-mile radius of my house in Northampton, Massachusetts, there are over 200 rail trails under development. This is the densest network in the United States, and much of this network is in New Hampshire. In fact, New Hampshire has more rail trails per capita than anywhere else in the United States; but much of this network is not yet developed, and in many places the trails are still largely undiscovered or used only in the winter for snowmobiling.

Charles's new book on New Hampshire's rail trails will lead you, too, to look at these special paths in a way you have probably never considered. The rich history he provides offers a glimpse into the way things used to be in the Granite State, but which is not all that far removed. The book's great maps will awaken curiosity as to where the paths go. That old bridge, which you have until now only seen from afar, now has a name and a purpose as to why it was there. This is the way a rail trail guide should be written, melding railroad history and description with trail descriptions. Along with first-class maps, this is certainly the best overall book ever done on rail trails in the United States.

Use this book to visit long forgotten places or use it to rediscover your own neighborhood. I guarantee you will never look at these paths the same way again.

CRAIG DELLA PENNA

January 2008

Acknowledgments

INSPIRATION for this book came from my first two trips on a New Hampshire rail trail, the Northern Rail Trail from Lebanon to Canaan and then on to Grafton. I was impressed by the scenery but had many questions and no source of answers. Why was there a railroad here? What are the lakes and rivers called? What town am I in? What should I be looking for? It soon became clear that there was no good source for this kind of information, and I decided to fill the gap.

I would like to thank my wife, Mardee, for supporting my rail trail obsession so I could complete this work. She was a wonderful help through the double stress of a demanding job and producing this book.

Several other individuals were especially helpful in creating the book. Jim Sindelar joined me on a large number of scouting trips and is rewarded by having his picture throughout the book. As amateur "railroad archeologists," we learned by doing. Jim's company and that of Bob Pugh, Alex Bernhard, and Jim Lerner made the scouting trips more fun. Craig Della Penna gave me encouragement at times when the effort seemed overwhelming. John Roy reviewed an early manuscript and offered elements of railroad lore that filled in missing links in my understanding. Ron and Diane Karr of Branch Line Press have kept me from blundering in both my English and my railroad knowledge, and they have produced an attractive volume. This has been a joint effort. Jennifer Codispoti provided information about the workings of the New Hampshire Bureau of Trails.

I felt that historical photographs were important to this book, and I am grateful to these individuals for showing me their collections and allowing me to use some of their pictures: Karen Booth of Karen Booth Photography, Pat Cutter and Ed Hiller of the Andover Historical Society, Ron Garceau of

Soo Nipi Publishing, Roland Goodbody of the University of New Hampshire Library, Frederick Nowell of the Boston & Maine Railroad Historical Society, Bobbie Nylander of the Hancock Historical Society, Richard Symmes of the Walker Collection at the Beverly (MA) Historical Society, Robert Welsch of the Lebanon Historical Society, and Dick Mackay, Brent Michiels, and the Karrs, who shared their fine private collections.

Several people reviewed early drafts of the manuscript and gave me excellent suggestions for improvements. These include Craig Della Penna, Bob Spoerl, Jennifer Codispoti, Lelia Mellen, Lou Barker, Jim Sindelar, and Amy Martin Webster.

Numerous other individuals have provided useful insights on particular trails. They include, in alphabetical order: Greg Bakos, Spencer Bennett, Alex Bernhard, Jim Bingham, Scott Bogle, Meade Cadot, Helen Closson, Jim Coffey, Rebecca Courser, Jay Crystal, Ken Cushing, Bertha Deveau, Stacy Doll, Paul Doolittle, Buddy Dougherty, John Doyle, Bill Elliott, Diane Fitzpatrick, Liz Fletcher, Marcia Gallaway, Chris Ganz, Dick Gassett, David Govatski, Hal Graham, Diane Hanley, Linda Harvey, Becky Hebert, Richard Holmes, Tom Jameson, Richard Jenkins, Tom Kerins, Sandra Lagueux, Odette Leclerc, Jim Lerner, Deborah Lievens, Valerie Maurer, Mike Micucci, Ron Mitchell, Christopher (Kit) Morgan, Karl Ronke, Rick Russack, Mark Samsel, Richard Silverberg, John St. Hilaire, John Summer, Richard Tichko, David Topham, Lowell Von Ruden, Barbara Watkins, Leigh Webb, and Eric Weiss. For those whom I have omitted, please accept my apologies.

Finally, let me thank the board of the Friends of the Northern Rail Trail in Merrimack County for their friendship and support. Bob Ward, Alex Bernhard, Myra Mayman, Peter Southworth, Tom Franz, Peter Crowell, Craig and Lindy Heim, and Phyllis Taylor have a diverse set of talents. This group is an example of the outstanding citizens action committees developing rail trails in New Hampshire.

Introduction

M<small>Y FRIENDS</small> and I had just finished scouting out a rail trail. Nearing the end of the day, we decided to ride our mountain bikes on the highway back to the car. Zoom… zoom… zoom the cars whizzed by—and we were reminded how much quieter and more peaceful it was on the rail trail. On summer days, the trails are shaded and cool, while the roads tend to be exposed and radiate heat from the black asphalt surface.

Where do you prefer to enjoy the outdoors?

Rail trails use the rights of way of abandoned railroad lines. They tell us a lot about life in nineteenth-century New Hampshire, when the state was growing up and railroads were its lifeline. Railroad passenger service brought immigrants to the growing mills, linked population centers with each other and with Boston, and brought tourists to the White Mountains and lakes regions. Freight trains brought coal and ice to communities and carried supplies and

Narrow dirt trails like the Granite Town Rail Trail are particularly scenic for walkers and bicyclists willing to go slowly over the bumps.

products to and from farms, factories, lumber mills, and textile mills. Following these trails, you can gain understanding of how New Hampshire farms, factories, and cities grew up, prospered, and then declined or changed.

Construction artifacts on or by the trails, such as expertly cut granite blocks for bridge supports, rock cuts, and major fills for viaducts, stand as monuments to the amazing construction projects from these 100- to 150-year-old ventures. Many railroad stations (often called "depots") still exist. Their varied architectural styles testify to the efforts of even small railroads that served rural communities like New Boston to show their modernity, high fashion, and commercial viability.

Most rail trails in New Hampshire are multiple-use pathways. Snowmobilers use them when covered with snow to travel large distances away from roads and to connect with other trails maintained by local snowmobile clubs. Bicycle riders use them to get exercise, see excellent scenery, and stay away from noisy and dangerous roads. Walkers and runners tend to use short sections of rail trails near their homes to get exercise in pleasant surroundings. Parents with

NEW HAMPSHIRE RAIL TRAILS

baby strollers and small children with tricycles traverse even shorter lengths of these linear parks, or greenways. Some commuters and school children find rail trails convenient alternative transportation routes when the weather cooperates.

School teachers enjoy bringing classes to rail trails to explore environmental concepts. These trails often traverse wetlands that display beaver handiwork and teem with various forms of life. Bird watchers and naturalists use trails to gain ready access to quiet wetland and woodland areas with different wildlife species from the ones in their backyards. Equestrian users ride their horses on them to connect with other riding trails. (Horseback riding is permitted as part of "non-motorized travel," except where the text explicitly mentions a prohibition.)

Users of All Terrain Vehicles (ATVs) and motorized trail bikes find rail trails to be good places to take their machines, where and when they are permitted. These off-highway recreational vehicles (OHRVs) are controversial. Many people consider their noise and speed to be incompatible with other uses. Abutting home owners usually consider them a noisy nuisance. Hence, they are prohibited from most, but not all, rail trails. OHRVs are plentiful on

Girls from the Andover Outing Club enjoy skate skiing on the Northern Rail Trail.
(Peter Southworth)

the few trails which permit them, such as the Sugar River and Fremont Branch Trails. In addition, New Hampshire currently allows winter OHRV use on most state-owned trails when they are covered with snow. A major legal and legislative challenge to this OHRV winter use is underway as this book goes to press.

In-line skaters practice their sport on paved rail trails. There are few paved trails in New Hampshire now, but major construction projects will add paved mileage in densely populated areas.

My own preference is to use a mountain bike, and this book reflects that bicycling bias. Some of the trails I describe in this book are quite long. Bicyclists riding these trails will usually want to park a car at both ends to avoid having to make a round trip. The most common use of rail trails, however, is walking, often with a dog. Walkers will generally want to take shorter sections of the long trails. The trail maps show most of the road crossings and intermediate access points to help plan such a stroll.

Overview of New Hampshire Rail Trails

For purposes of grouping railroads and trails geographically, I divided the state into five regions: Southwest, Southeast, Central West, Central East, and North. (This choice of regions does not correspond to the areas covered by the state's regional planning commissions, as the railroads inevitably crossed those boundaries.) The Bureau of Trails considers some railroad corridors that still have track or rough ballast rock on the right way to be trails even though they can only be used in the winter when there is adequate snow cover. In this book, I give detailed descriptions and ratings only for trails available for four-season use. However, some winter-use-only trail sections and some as yet unimproved sections of rail corridor have the potential to become four-season trails, and you will find discussions of these proposed trails in several chapters.

The state's rail trails vary widely in trail surface characteristics, scenery, and ownership. A few trails are paved; most are not. Surface characteristics and condition are quite varied on the unpaved trails. You may find dirt, stone dust, cinders, sand, and tree roots—sometimes all on the same trail! Trail width can vary from fourteen feet down to just a few feet. Water, brush, road fill barriers, and incursion obstacles may block your way.

Part of the rail trail charm in New Hampshire is the "Live Free or Die" spirit of making the paths available without requirements to create "ideal" trails.

This is a refreshing change from the experience I had when living in Massachusetts, where endless hearings and engineering studies had to be completed before any trail work could proceed. Trail surface quality and ease of passage are important to users, however. Since you and I may have different views on the level of adventure we consider fun, I have developed the following trail condition rating scheme.

Trail Condition Rating	Meaning	Users (where allowed)	Example Trails
★ ★ ★ ★ ★	Smooth asphalt surface or well-graded and rolled hardpack	Everyone except equestrians when paved; everyone except inline skaters when not paved	Windham, Northern in Andover
★ ★ ★ ★	Generally good surface with some bumps due to gravel and mild ruts	Similar to 5-star, but less comfortable; bicyclists should have fat tires.	Hillsborough
★ ★ ★	Obstructions from rocks, tree roots, mud, wet spots, and sand make the trail adventurous. Some loving care would correct "roller coaster" stretches.	Bicyclists in good physical shape who enjoy the challenge; hikers should watch their footing.	Granite Town, Freemont Branch
★ ★	Not developed as a formal trail, but you can get through. Trees, rocks, pools, and earth barriers make it a real challenge.	Primarily for railroad enthusiasts interested in tracing the right of way.	Londonderry stretch of Manchester & Lawrence
★	Impassible. Bridges are missing, brush or swampy areas block the right of way, or houses and roads took it over.	Mentioned, but not included as trail descriptions in this edition; future construction may make these into usable trails.	Manchester & Lawrence north of Beech Street; bog section of Piscataquog

I use the term "roller coaster" to describe undulating stretches of dirt trail where hills and valleys have formed due to vehicle use.

Example of a roller coaster stretch of trail

Scenery is as important as trail riding comfort. Mountain views, free-flowing rivers, scenic wetlands, and interesting cultural artifacts provide much of the pleasure in using rail trails. Conversely, trash and the back side of industrial buildings are much less appealing. The scenery rating scale will help you select scenic outings.

Scenery Rating	Meaning	Example Trails
★ ★ ★ ★ ★	Outstanding views of rivers, lakes, wetlands, mountains, open fields, and woods; away from roads; interesting artifacts from the railroad days, such as hand-cut granite masonry work, surviving depots, railroad bridges, and abandoned factories. Trail is attractive and blends into surroundings.	Ammonoosuc west of Lisbon, Northern, Cheshire, Fremont Branch, Profile
★ ★ ★ ★	Pleasant woods and wetlands, but less spectacular scenery. Some mileage markers and bridges, but few signs of the railroad's past. Roads nearby.	New Boston, Henniker Junction Tour
★ ★ ★	Open but flat, uninteresting scenery; roads usually in view.	Ammonoosuc east of Lisbon
★ ★	Mixture of trashy settings and more open country. Needs work to improve the appearance.	Londonderry stretch of Manchester & Lawrence
★	Built-up industrial area with trash	Salem stretch of Manchester & Lawrence line

Privately Owned Trails

Many rail trails in New Hampshire are either totally or partly on private property. Snowmobile clubs have been proactive at working with landowners to get permission for winter use. By contrast, very little effort has gone into making similar arrangements for non-winter use. A key objective of this book is to stimulate volunteer groups to improve and maintain rail trails for spring, summer, and fall use. This includes working with landowners of privately owned stretches in a manner similar to the snowmobile clubs. In return for generously allowing public use, landowners get nicely maintained trails to use themselves and to increase the value of their properties. Groups like the Winnipesaukee River Trail Association and the town of Milford have been very successful at obtaining trail use easements.

Some of the most interesting rail trails in New Hampshire are on private property. Often the trails are not currently posted against trespass. However, in writing this book, I have attempted to avoid describing privately owned trails unless there are specific indications that the trail is open to the public. I may have made some mistakes where ownership is not clear. Remember: permission to use privately owned trails can be revoked at any time. If anyone is a nuisance, the dreaded "no trespassing" signs will deny access for us all!

Permitted Uses

The subject of permitted uses of rail trails is complex and sometimes controversial. Particularly contentious is whether off-highway recreational vehicles (OHRVs), a category including all terrain vehicles (ATVs) and motorized trail bikes, should be allowed. New Hampshire laws specify how each state-owned trail may be used. The New Hampshire Bureau of Trails summarizes these permissions on their web site under "Recreational Rail Trails." OHRVs are often prohibited from trails not owned by the state.

In order to simplify the exposition in this book, I use the term "non-motorized travel" to include such activities as walking, bicycling, horseback riding, and cross-country skiing. I try to be explicit about OHRV and snowmobile use. But conditions change. Check out the Trails Bureau web site and signage on the trail itself to make a final determination. And don't be a scofflaw by engaging in prohibited uses. Even bicycles can be prohibited from sensitive environments.

Historical Overview

After the War of 1812, America was on the move. Numerous turnpikes were constructed throughout New Hampshire. Stage coaches like the famous Concord Coach, produced by the Abbot Downing Company, made for more regular transportation in relative comfort. Completion of the Erie Canal in 1825 led to locks and river travel on the Connecticut and Merrimack rivers.

Both river travel and horseback over rough roads were insufficient for the growing travel demands in New Hampshire. Small swift-flowing streams and mountainous terrain did not lend themselves to an extensive canal system, and travel speed on roads was limited to about five miles per hour. Then a new technology arrived, with a startling change in the speed of transportation.

Railroads sprang up in the 1830s to serve the major cities of Boston, New York, and Philadelphia. Railroad networks expanded from Boston and Worcester into New Hampshire starting in 1838. Railroad fever then overtook the

NEW HAMPSHIRE BUREAU OF TRAILS

The state agency responsible for trails, including rail trails, is the New Hampshire Bureau of Trails (commonly called "Trails Bureau"), part of the Division of Parks and Recreation in the Department of Resources and Economic Development (DRED). The Department of Transportation (DOT) administers most state-owned railroad corridors but has agreed to let the Trails Bureau manage most of them as trails until other transportation needs supersede.

In typical New Hampshire fashion, there is not much state money for trails, so the Trails Bureau works closely with volunteer groups for trail construction and maintenance. It provides grants for groups supporting both motorized and non-motorized trail use. The bureau's Grant In Aid program provides support for snowmobile and ATV clubs to construct and maintain trails. This money comes from registration fees, and you will often see signs on trails saying "Your registration fees at work." In addition, the Trails Bureau manages the federal Recreational Trail Program, which provides grants to groups improving trails for all categories of use.

The bureau removes trash and repairs trails that are damaged by misuse or weather conditions. Their web site, www.NHTrails.org, publishes permitted uses on each trail. They construct barrier gates to keep cars and trucks off the trail, open them in the winter for snowmobiles and OHRVs, and close them again when the snow melts in the spring.

Volunteer groups must coordinate their activities on state-owned trails with the Bureau of Trails.

Other states use bollards (metal posts), but New Hampshire uses striped gates to keep cars and trucks off their trails. The sign behind the gate lists permitted uses on the trail.

state; every hamlet wanted a connection. Main-line railroads like the Concord and the Northern became the foundation for branch lines like the Concord & Claremont and the Portsmouth & Concord.

A railroad required two things to proceed: a charter from the state legislature and money for construction, locomotives, and equipment. Apparently the two were connected, as "gifts" were frequently given to members of the legislature. Armed with a charter, a railroad could set the route where it wanted. After surveyors determined a route, advance men would negotiate damages (compensation) to landowners. Then the work crews would follow along the surveyed line.

These early railroads were built very quickly, since they needed to start service promptly to generate revenue for stockholders. They were typically constructed using cheap immigrant (often Irish) labor. The Northern Railroad took less than two years to build its sixty-mile line from Concord to Lebanon. Masonry work for bridges and culverts was done with beautifully fitted, hand-cut granite, usually quarried from along or near the railroad bed. Given that trains require a grade of no more than 2%, New Hampshire lines required frequent cuts and fills through hilly countryside to level the routes. Cuts were particularly laborious through the state's renowned granite. They required hand drilling a hole in the rock, filling the hole with black powder, setting off an explosion, and hoping a lot of rock would flake off. These steps were repeated for months to complete major cuts. Fills required transporting large amounts of rock, gravel, and dirt by railroad car and shoveling out the material to build up the railroad grade. Where a ravine was too substantial to cross with a fill, the railroads used trestle and truss bridges. Some, like the Greenville Bridge, were very impressive.

In the second half of the nineteenth century, additional railroads came into being and quickly covered the state. Perhaps because mortar was cheaper and easier to obtain, the masonry work was rougher; instead of having to fit granite blocks perfectly, a rough fit sufficed because the cracks were filled with mortar. Competition between railroads was brutal. Some thrived. Some made no money and were taken over by their more successful neighbors. Changes in ownership and name occurred so frequently that it is difficult to know what to call each line today. Fortunately, in his well researched book, *The Rail Lines of Northern New England*, Robert M. Lindsell did an excellent job of deciding the most classic name for each line, so I have followed his lead in most cases.

Two short-lived developments appeared around the end of the nineteenth century: logging railroads and electric lines. The logging railroads, located in the northern part of the state, supported massive clear-cutting timber harvests. The electric lines were commuter streetcars moving people around urban areas, including Keene, Nashua, Manchester, Concord, Portsmouth, Laconia, and Berlin. The logging railroads were abandoned after a few years, when the forests were stripped. Trails on those lines are mostly in the White Mountain National Forest. The electric lines gave way to buses. Little remains of them, but you will see references to short stretches in Goffstown and Londonderry in this guide.

At the end of the nineteenth century, the Boston & Maine Railroad succeeded in taking over almost all of the other railroads in the state. By World War I, the railroad system was to New Hampshire what the road network is today—the primary means people used to travel to their destinations and ship goods.

In the twentieth century, the railroads went through a long period of decline as cars, buses, and trucks took over the traffic. Even the mighty Boston & Maine ran into financial trouble, and Guilford Transportation (recently rebranded as Pan Am Railways) acquired it in 1983. Railroads that were abandoned early tended to be sold off to abutting landowners, although a few towns like Mason, Milford, and New Boston were able to preserve the rights of way as trails. Railroads that gave up toward the end of the century were bought up by the state of New Hampshire using Federal Transportation Enhancement grants. These are the corridors that have become the state's major rail trails.

Removing Northern Railroad rails in Andover in 2000
(Dick Mackay)

One common misconception is that conversion of a railroad bed to a trail is anti-railroad. In reality, if no company wants to run trains, and the right of way is not converted to trail, it is likely to be cut up, given to adjacent landowners, and built upon. Preserving intact railroad corridors allows for future revival of rail use.

You can help improve the state's rail trails. Many are still works in progress. Each trail presents special issues, from handling private property obstructions to obtaining permits for construction. Volunteer groups (see Helpful Organizations chapter), working with local, regional, and state authorities, catalyze the efforts to build and maintain the trails. This is exciting activity, working with great people, and I heartily encourage your participation.

Maps

It is easy to get confused when exploring rail trails. Questions like the following arise: "Where did that railroad go?" "How was it connected to the rest of the system?" "Where should I park to ride or walk the trail?" It took considerable effort to design maps that answer those questions accurately and informatively. After much trial and error, I developed four types of maps to keep trail users well oriented.

The region maps provide overviews showing how the various railroads linked (or competed) to provide service for each of the five New Hampshire regions. Railroad lines that still have tracks in place are shown as solid lines with cross hatches. Abandoned railroad lines are shown as dotted lines. Some abandoned lines, like the Northern Railroad, have rail trails. Others, like the Eastern Railroad, have sections that are candidates for trails. Abandoned railroads with a **boldfaced** name (e.g., the Monadnock Railroad) are described in detail, with history and overview of current and possible trails. Numbers along their routes correspond to the rail trails described in the book and indicate how the trails are sequenced within the region. Railroad names in regular type denote lines that do not have rail trail possibilities. All railroads are named using historic titles, usually the first company to obtain a state charter for the line.

The Railroad maps are simple schematics showing the start and end of the line and all the stations in between. In addition, they show connecting railroads as dotted lines (abandoned) or solid lines with cross hatches (active).

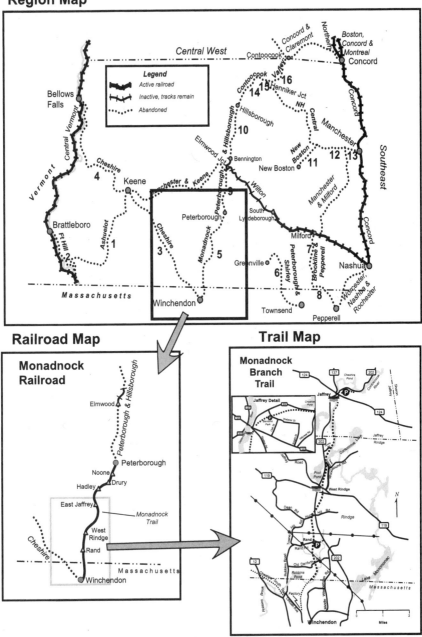

Region Map

Legend
- Active railroad
- Inactive, tracks remain
- Abandoned

Central West
Contoocook
Concord & Claremont
Northern
Boston, Concord & Montreal
Concord
Contoocook Valley
Henniker Jct
16
15
14
NH
Bellows Falls
Central Vermont
Hillsborough
10
Elmwood Jct
Peterborough & Hillsborough
Bennington
New Boston
11
Manchester
12
13
Southeast
Cheshire
4
Keene
Manchester & Keene
Wilton
New Boston
Manchester & Milford
Concord
Vermont
Peterborough
South Lyndeborough
Milford
Brattleboro
Ft Hill
Ashuelot
1
Cheshire
3
Monadnock
5
Greenville
Peterborough & Shirley
6
7
Brookline
Pepperell
Nashua
Worcester, Nashua & Rochester
2
Winchendon
Townsend
8
Pepperell
Massachusetts

Railroad Map

Monadnock Railroad

Peterborough & Hillsborough
Elmwood
Peterborough
Noone
Drury
Hadley
East Jaffrey
Monadnock Trail
West Rindge
Cheshire
Rand
Massachusetts
Winchendon

Trail Map

Monadnock Branch Trail

124
137
202
Cheshire Pond
Contoocook River
Jaffrey
Jaffrey Detail
Park
124
Jaffrey Rindge
202
119
Pool Pond
West Rindge
Dean Rd
Rindge
119
N
123
Rand
Rand Rd
202
Old Danforth
Robbins Pond
Lake Monomonoc
Factory
Massachusetts
Winchendon
0 1 2
Miles

Rectangles within these maps show the areas covered by each of the trail maps for this railroad.

Trail maps detail individual rail trails along each railroad corridor. They clarify access points, points of interest, and landmarks indicating where you are on the trail. Where possible, these maps show names of the stations on the railroad. These help connect the trail map locations to the larger-scale railroad maps and are also clues for where to look for signs of former depots. Sometimes there is no longer any sign of railroad activity at these locations.

Detail maps of complex areas on the trail maps are included with some trail descriptions. These are particularly useful to show difficult-to-find trailheads.

Developed parking areas appear on trail and detail maps as 🅿. Turnouts that accommodate less than three cars are not shown as parking areas. Most road crossings of trails have room for one or two cars to park off the road.

Trail maps and descriptions sometimes mention "culverts." This term is used in this book and by rail trail developers according to its dictionary meaning of "conduit or drain to carry a stream under a road or railroad bed," as well as for the large pipes and concrete boxes that have been adapted for use as tunnels for trails to cross under roads.

Photographs

The contemporary photographs in this book illustrate the scenery, trail conditions, and problematic access points of the trails. All were taken by the author, unless otherwise noted. Historic photographs were selected to show how an important location on the railroad looked when the railroad was in operation. For example, when looking at the remaining Greenville Bridge piers, it is helpful to see a picture of the long bridge that formerly crossed over the Souhegan River and highway on these piers.

The surfaces of some New Hampshire rail trails are imperfect, but the scenery is well worth the effort to walk around obstacles like this wet spot on the Portsmouth Branch Trail.

Trails Overview

Trail No.	Trail Name	Miles	Trail Condition	Scenery Rating
	Southwest Region			
1	Ashuelot Recreational Trail	21	★★★★	★★★★★
2	Fort Hill Recreational Trail	9	★★★	★★★
3	Cheshire South Trail	20	★★★★	★★★★★
4	Cheshire North Trail	14	★★★★	★★★★★
5	Monadnock Recreational Trail	7.5	★★★★	★★★★
6	Mason-Greenville Rail Trail	9	★★★★	★★★★
7	Granite Town Rail Trail	6	★★★	★★★★★
8	Potanipo Railroad Trail	3	★★★	★★★★
9	Peterborough Trail	9	★★★★	★★★★
10	Hillsborough Recreational Trail	8	★★★★	★★★★
11	New Boston Rail Trail	5	★★★	★★★★
12	Goffstown Rail Trail	6.5	★★★	★★★
13	Piscataquog Trail	1.5	★★★	★★★
14	Contoocook Fishing Access	2.4	★★★	★★★★
15	Henniker Junction Tour	2.3	★★★	★★★★
16	Hopkinton Dam to Former Bridge	2.1	★★★	★★★★
	Southeast Region			
1	South Manchester Trailway	1	★★★★★	★★★★
2	Londonderry Rail Trail	5.4	★★	★★★
3	Derry Rail Trail	3.6	★★★★	★★★★
4	Windham Rail Trail	4.1	★★★★★	★★★★★
5	Nashua River Rail Trail: New Hampshire Extension	1	★★★★★	★★★
6	Windham Greenway	2	★★★	★★★★
7	Fremont Branch Trail	18.5	★★★	★★★★★
8	Portsmouth Branch Trail: Massabesic-to-Raymond	12	★★★	★★★★★
	Raymond-to-Rockingham Jct.	13	★★★	★★★★
	Central West Region			
1	Sugar River Rail Trail	9	★★★★	★★★★★
2	Northern Rail Trail, Grafton County	25	★★★★	★★★★★
3	Northern Rail Trail, Merrimack County: Andover 4-Season Trail	5.7	★★★★★	★★★★★
4	Winnipesaukee River Trail	3.1	★★★★	★★★★★
5	Warren Recreational Trail	6	★★★★	★★★★
6	North Haverhill–Woodsville Trail	3.6	★★★★	★★★

Central East Region				
1	Farmington Recreational Trail	8.2	★★★	★★★
2	Bridge Falls/Cotton Valley Trail	6	★★★	★★★★★
3	Wakefield Heritage Trail	0.7	★★★	★★★★
North Region				
1	Ammonoosuc Rail Trail:			
	Woodsville-to-Lisbon	9.7	★★★	★★★★★
	Lisbon-to-Littleton	9.1	★★★	★★★
2	Presidential Range Trail:			
	Pondicherry Section	3.7	★★★	★★★★★
	Israel River Section	6.4	★★★	★★★★
	Moose River Section	8.6	★★★	★★★★★
	Androscoggin Section	6	★★★	★★★
3	Profile Recreational Trail	2	★★★	★★★★★
4	Upper Coos Recreational Trail	8.7	★★	★★★★★

Warnings

Like any outdoor physical activity, use of rail trails brings the possibility of collisions, crashes, and onset of physical ailments. Road crossings and trails with a trail condition rating of three stars or less are particularly hazardous. This book is as up-to-date as of January 2008 as the author could make it, but it may contain errors. Trails will change over time with construction and maintenance (or lack thereof), new hazards may arise, and permitted uses may change. Obey sign postings and avoid going on active railroad tracks, as it is both dangerous and prohibited by state law. When you ride or walk these trails, you take full responsibility for your own safety.

Map Key

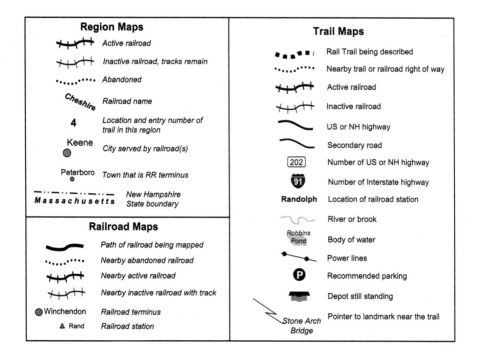

Region Maps

┼┼┼┼	Active railroad
┼┼┼┼	Inactive railroad, tracks remain
••••••••••	Abandoned
Cheshire	Railroad name
4	Location and entry number of trail in this region
Keene ●	City served by railroad(s)
Peterboro ○	Town that is RR terminus
— ·· — · — ·· — **Massachusetts**	New Hampshire State boundary

Railroad Maps

~~	Path of railroad being mapped
••••••••	Nearby abandoned railroad
┼┼┼┼	Nearby active railroad
┼┼┼┼	Nearby inactive railroad with track
● Winchendon	Railroad terminus
▲ Rand	Railroad station

Trail Maps

■ ■ ▪ ▪ ▪ ▫	Rail Trail being described
••••••••••	Nearby trail or railroad right of way
┼┼┼┼	Active railroad
┼┼┼┼	Inactive railroad
～～	US or NH highway
～～	Secondary road
[202]	Number of US or NH highway
🛡91	Number of Interstate highway
Randolph	Location of railroad station
～v～	River or brook
Robbins Pond	Body of water
•—●—•	Power lines
Ⓟ	Recommended parking
▬	Depot still standing
⟍ Stone Arch Bridge	Pointer to landmark near the trail

NEW HAMPSHIRE RAIL TRAILS

Southwest Region

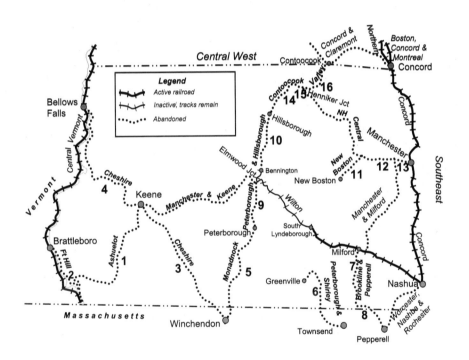

THE Southwest Region extends from the Connecticut River (Vermont border) east to the Merrimack River and from the Massachusetts border north to Concord and Bellows Falls, VT.

The eleven highlighted abandoned railroads in this region traversed what is now semi-rural countryside, making one wonder how much more industry there was in the nineteenth century to make this construction worthwhile.

The western half of the Wilton line would make an outstanding rail trail. The tracks are still there, but no trains.

Their corridors have excellent trails, as well as opportunities for new trails, as described in this section.

Keene was big enough to support three railroads, none of which have survived. The Pathways for Keene organization has done an outstanding job of creating and maintaining trails on the former Cheshire, Ashuelot, and Fort Hill lines.

Two successful railroads followed the major rivers: the Central Vermont and the Concord. These are now operated by the New England Central/Amtrak and by Pan Am Railways/New England Southern, respectively.

The Wilton line is the only other southwest region railroad that still has track. With the recent demise of the Wilton Scenic Railroad, there are no current railroad operations west of South Lyndeborough. The Bennington-to-South Lyndeborough stretch could make an outstanding rail trail if the state Department of Transportation gives up trying to run trains there.

NEW HAMPSHIRE RAIL TRAILS

The Manchester & Milford Railroad was abandoned long ago (1926). The right of way is still recognizable in a few sections, but privately owned. I have not discovered any trail opportunities on this corridor.

One railroad, the Worcester, Nashua & Rochester, has a small segment in the southwest region. The stretch between Nashua and Pepperell, MA, contains a one-mile extension of the Nashua River Rail Trail, which begins in Ayer, MA. Most of the WN&R's New Hampshire course is in the southeast region, so the description of that mile of trail (SE5) appears in the next section.

PATHWAYS FOR KEENE

Keene has an active group devoted to development and use of bicycling and walking routes in the city of Keene and Cheshire County. Called Pathways for Keene, it has produced an excellent map called the **Bicycle and Pedestrian Guide**. One side shows practical ways to navigate the trails and streets of Keene. The other side shows Cheshire County bicycle routes, including the Cheshire, Ashuelot, and Fort Hill Rail Trails. To order the **Bicycle and Pedestrian Guide** or to learn how you can help improve Cheshire County trails, go to their web site: www.tlaorg.org/pathways.

Ashuelot Railroad

East Northfield, MA, to Keene
Built: 1849–51
Abandoned: 1983

The Ashuelot Railroad was one of the early lines in New Hampshire, completed in 1851. It connected the northern limit of the Connecticut River Railroad (not shown on the map) in East Northfield, MA, with the Cheshire Railroad in Keene. The Cheshire had been completed shortly before, in 1849.

The railroad followed the circuitous route of the Ashuelot River to avoid extensive tunnels, fills, and cuts. It was therefore easy for it to handle freight from the manufacturing plants located on the river.

Revenues were small, and the railroad was leased to other railroads, including the Connecticut River and Cheshire, until finally ending up in the Boston & Maine Railroad's hands as the Ashuelot Branch in 1893. After the line was abandoned in 1983, the state of New Hampshire purchased the right of way from Dole Junction to Keene and made that entire length into a rail trail.

Pathways for Keene is investigating the possibility of continuing the trail south from Dole Junction to Northfield, MA, to link up with the historic Schell Bridge across the Connecticut River.

SW1. Ashuelot Recreational Trail

Dole Junction to Keene, 21 miles

Trail condition: ★ ★ ★ ★ Easy going except for a wet area under a road overpass in West Swanzey that may be bypassed. Highway and new rotary cut the trail in Keene.

Scenery: ★ ★ ★ ★ Good views of the Ashuelot River, ruins of old mills by the river, covered bridges, and railroad artifacts.

Permitted uses: Non-motorized travel year-round; snowmobiles, ATVs, and motorized trail bikes in winter when snow-covered.

Right of way owned by: State of New Hampshire.

Maintained by: Trails Bureau, Pathways for Keene, Swanzey Bike Path Committee, Winchester Trail Riders, and Keene Sno-Riders.

ACCESS

This twenty-one-mile trail makes an excellent day's bicycle trip if you plant a car at each end. There is a large parking area at Dole Junction on the west side of Route 63. The Fort Hill Trail begins at the parking lot, whereas the Ashuelot Trail starts across the road. Frequent road crossings offer other access opportunities for those who wish to explore shorter sections of the trail. If you want to explore a few miles on foot, the section along the Ashuelot River between Depot Street and Gunn Mountain Road in Ashuelot is the most interesting.

On the Keene end of the trail (Map 3), the 2007 construction of a rotary where Routes 12 and 101 join Route 10 altered a very dangerous highway crossing. With the rotary close to the trail, crossing the highway is now prohibited. The Department of Transportation plans to construct a trail bridge; however, until that happens, you may park a car near the Keene/Swanzey border. A planned parking area on Matthews Road will be the best place when it is finished. There is also limited parking near the Cresson Covered Bridge, where the trail intersects Sawyers Crossing Road.

There is no special trail parking for the half mile of trail north of the highway.

DESCRIPTION

This trail has a remarkable diversity of scenery, making it one of my favorites. The trail is close to the Ashuelot River much of the way, with river character

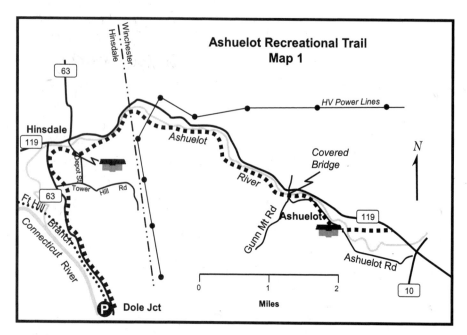

shifting from rapids to calm meandering flows. Woodsy stretches have a remote feeling. Old mill buildings testify to New Hampshire's nineteenth-century commerce. Railroad depots, covered bridges, and some interesting homes give some feeling for the energy and Yankee spirit that propelled the region. The scenery includes newer housing and a speedway, bringing you back to modern times.

The dirt trail is well maintained for mountain biking. It follows Route 63 for the first mile north from Dole Junction, and then goes into the woods and through some rock cuts. After making a big turn eastward, you come upon the Hinsdale depot and freight house. It has been nicely renovated as a home by a railroad buff who keeps some old rolling stock behind it.

East of Hinsdale, the trail follows an attractive stretch of the Ashuelot River, which drops through gentle rapids. The river gradient supported mills using water power. You pass several old mill sites with their railroad sidings. One derelict brick plant is a particularly impressive ruin, and its river frontage offers a nice stopping place for lunch. Avoid the temptation to trespass in this dangerous ruin.

About a half mile past the Ashuelot Covered Bridge, the Ashuelot depot marks the end of the water-powered plants. The depot still stands, but its sorry shape begs for someone to restore it to glory.

This ruin of a factory building was once a thriving part of New Hampshire industry.

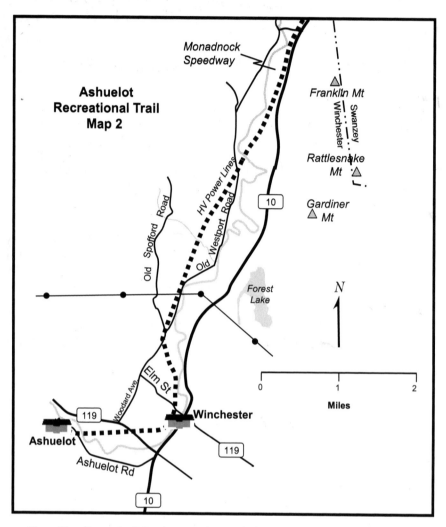

Ashuelot Recreational Trail Map 2

Monadnock Speedway

Franklin Mt

Winchester Swanzey

Rattlesnake Mt

Gardiner Mt

10

Old Spofford Road

HV Power Lines

Old Westport Road

Forest Lake

N

0   1   2

Miles

Elm St

Woodard Ave

119

Winchester

Ashuelot

119

Ashuelot Rd

10

Near Elm Street in Winchester, the trail changes character. The river loses its drop, becoming a meandering stream through wetlands. The trail crosses more roads, and you have to put up with power lines at your side. However, this section offers pleasing views of the hills to the east. The second railroad bridge over the river displays the placid river in contrast to the rapids downstream.

You come next to the Monadnock Speedway. It is a stark reminder of what caused the downfall of the railroads.

West Swanzey contains the first of two big obstacles on the ride. Main Street crosses the right of way on a small bridge. When I rode the trail, there were

Abandoned and forlorn, the Ashuelot Depot stands in dramatic contrast to the nicely restored depot at Hinsdale.

muddy stretches leading up to the bridge and two inches of water on the trail just north of the bridge. My feet got soaked. Apparently, this is the usual situation in this poorly drained spot. A better alternative is to take a loop on Homestead Avenue around this area.

Continuing north from West Swanzey, the trail crosses a third railroad bridge with more river views. At Sawyers Crossing Road, be sure to take a side trip to the east to admire the Cresson Covered Bridge. It has an unusual truss system of cables fastened to long beams under the bridge.

North of the covered bridge, you come first to the Keene State College stadium, then to the prohibited highway crossing of Routes 101 and 12. The New Hampshire Department of Transportation plans to build a pedestrian and snowmobile bridge here in 2009. This is critically important for both Keene State students and trail users. After completion of the bridge, you will cross over the busy highway and then come to a fourth railroad bridge over the Ashuelot River. Shortly after, the trail comes to an end.

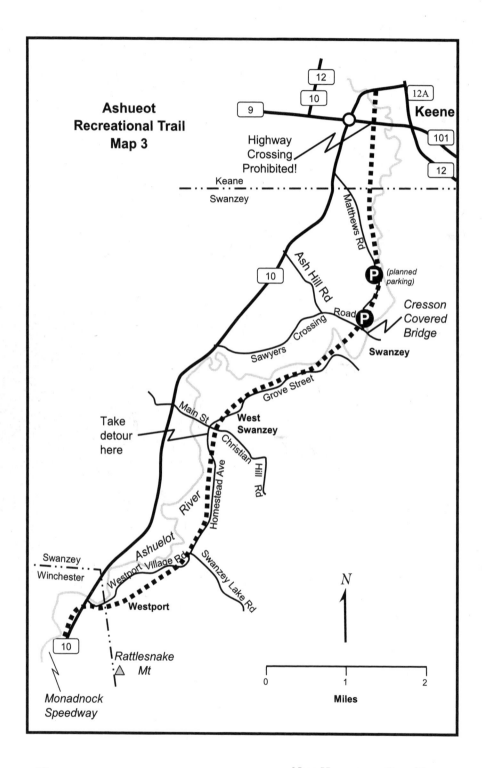

Ashueot Recreational Trail Map 3

Highway Crossing Prohibited!

Keane
Swanzey

Keene

Cresson Covered Bridge

Swanzey

West Swanzey

Take detour here

Swanzey
Winchester

Westport

Rattlesnake Mt

Monadnock Speedway

(planned parking)

N

0   1   2
Miles

The Cresson and Ashuelot Covered Bridges are close to the trail.

Fort Hill Branch

Dole Junction to Brattleboro, VT
Built: 1913
Abandoned:1983

The Boston & Maine Railroad built the Fort Hill Branch in 1912–13 to avoid reliance on the Central Vermont between South Vernon and Brattleboro. The two railroads jointly operated the Connecticut River line. (Don't confuse this with the railroad of the same name from Springfield, MA, to East Northfield, MA, that the B&M had taken control of in 1893.) Some trains took the B&M Fort Hill track east of the Connecticut River, while others took the CV track west of the river.

The southern end of this line took advantage of the Ashuelot Branch's bridge over the Connecticut River at South Vernon. To connect with Brattleboro, the Fort Hill Branch required a new bridge and a causeway over a flooded section of the river. A remote location called Dole Junction was chosen as the switching point from the Ashuelot Branch.

There was only one station on the line: Fort Hill, named for an Indian fort. There is no trace of it today. It must have been given up early; there is no mention of it on the 1935 USGS topographic map.

As the last railroad line built in New Hampshire, construction details on the Fort Hill Branch were not as picturesque as on the older Ashuelot and Cheshire lines nearby. Instead of beautifully carved granite masonry, the B&M used a lot of concrete in the bridges and culverts.

The B&M kept the Fort Hill Branch in good repair until 1983, when the last remnants of the Ashuelot Branch in Keene were abandoned. After the Connecticut River bridge at South Vernon failed in 1970, the Fort Hill Branch became the only way for trains to reach Keene.

The state of New Hampshire bought the Fort Hill Branch, Ashuelot Branch, and Cheshire Branch rights of way in 1984. John Summer of Pathways for Keene convinced the state to buy the railroad bridge to Brattleboro as well. He is working to get the bridge decked and a trailhead constructed on the Vermont side of the river.

SW2. Fort Hill Recreational Trail

Dole Junction to Brattleboro railroad bridge, Hinsdale, 9 miles.

Trail condition: ★ ★ ★ North end is overgrown, some wet spots, and trees across the trail; the Connecticut River bridge is undecked and unusable at this time.

Scenery: ★ ★ ★ Two interesting railroad bridges, views of the Connecticut River at a dam pool, power lines, and the Vermont Yankee Nuclear Power Plant in Vernon.

Permitted uses: Non-motorized travel year-round; snowmobiles, ATVs, and motorized trail bikes allowed in winter when snow-covered.

Right of way owned by: State of New Hampshire.

Maintained by: Trails Bureau, Pathways for Keene, and Pisgah Mountain Trail Riders.

ACCESS

Access is problematic on the north end. Since the Connecticut River bridge is impassible, you cannot get on the trail from the Vermont side. Near the bridge on the New Hampshire side, the trail is close to Route 119, but down a steep, brushy bank. You can make it down a rough path behind the Citgo station on Route 119, but the first decent access is about a mile south of the bridge using a path from a picnic area marked with a picnic table sign.

At the southern end, the Trails Bureau maintains a parking area at Dole Junction. Alternative access points near the southern end are from River Road and Prospect Street. There is decent parking at both of these locations.

This sign is the only notice for the picnic area off Route 119.

DESCRIPTION

I was really looking forward to scouting this trail. With views of the Connecticut River and some interesting bridges, it sounded great. Was I disappointed! The dam on the peninsula north of Stebbins Island backs up the river, forming a wide stagnant pool. Views across the river feature power lines and the Vermont Yankee Nuclear Power Plant. The undecked Connecticut River bridge was too dangerous to cross, and the Ashuelot River bridge had been damaged by fire and was still under repair when I scouted in September 2006. The trail was overgrown north of the Citgo station, making it necessary to plow through weeds that were three feet high. Still, with brush clearing and decking of the bridge over the Connecticut, this trail would be worth exploring on a summer excursion.

The parking area at Dole Junction is just north of the historic railroad junction. The Fort Hill and Ashuelot rights of way are overgrown to the south, so there appears to be no way to get to the Massachusetts border along the railroad grade.

Heading north from the parking lot, you get a good view of the river, pass a town dump site, and then come to the Ashuelot River bridge. This is a solidly built bridge based on steel I-beams on masonry piers. Unfortunately, an arson-

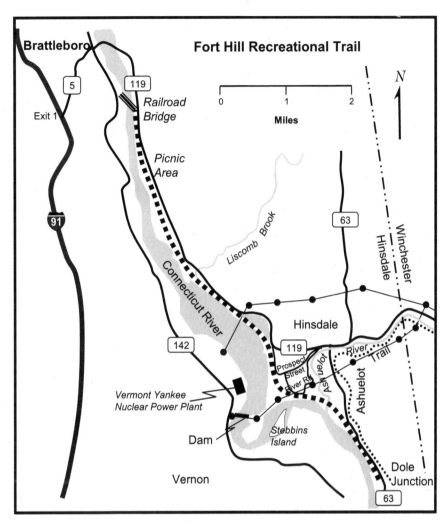

Fort Hill Recreational Trail

Brattleboro

5

119

Railroad Bridge

Exit 1

Picnic Area

91

Connecticut River

Liscomb Brook

63

Winchester Hinsdale

Hinsdale

142

119

River Trail

Prospect Street

Ashuelot River Rd

Ashuelot

Vermont Yankee Nuclear Power Plant

Dam

Stebbins Island

Vernon

Dole Junction

63

0   1   2

Miles

N

ist tried to burn the bridge down and did manage to damage the railroad ties near the southern end. The Trails Bureau repaired the bridge in late 2006.

After passing a crumbling road overpass, you come to a New England Power Company access driveway (closed to the public) and the River Road access and parking. The trail crosses a large culvert that was rebuilt in cement in 1950. It then traverses the causeway built for the railroad over the flooded river. The trail surface is very good here, and there are views through birch trees of the bay to the east.

Further along you pass a driveway out to an island with towers for the northern set of high voltage lines. From there the trail continues along the

The Connecticut River bridge still has rails, and gaps between ties make crossing dangerous.

Connecticut River with few hazards other than a muddy area. The Liscomb Brook crossing uses a more picturesque stone and concrete culvert.

The trail quality deteriorates after the picnic area access and may be overgrown with weeds north of the Citgo path. Apparently this stretch gets mowed in time for winter snowmobiling, but nobody takes responsibility for clearing the trail for four-season use. Still, it is worth making your way up to the Connecticut River bridge.

The bridge is substantial, having been designed to allow expansion to double track. With commanding views of the river, it should be the highlight of this trail. However, it is undecked and has big gaps between the railroad ties. Hence, it is unavailable for snowmobiles or bicycles and is dangerous to walk upon. If some group takes on the project of decking the bridge for pedestrian use, it would be the main attraction for this trail.

Cheshire Railroad

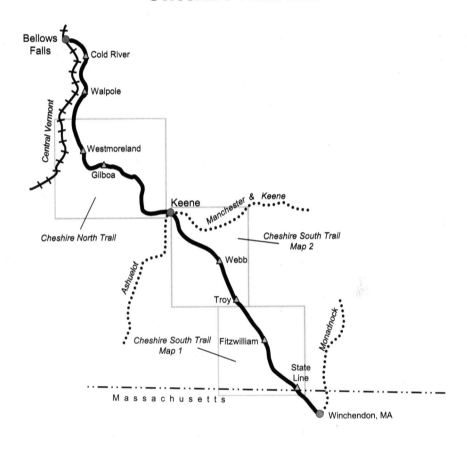

Winchendon, MA, to Bellows Falls, VT
Built: 1845–49
Abandoned: 1972

New Hampshire granted Keene businessmen a charter for the Cheshire Railroad in 1844. Named for the county, it provided a route to the northwest from Fitchburg, MA, and served the factories in Keene. The line was completed northward to Keene in 1848 and to Bellows Falls in 1849. Manufacturers in Keene shipped woolens, shoes, furniture, bicycles, automobiles, and silverware.

At first the line was successful, but competition gradually eroded its profitability, and it was taken over by the Fitchburg Railroad in 1890. The Fitchburg, Cheshire, and Rutland Railroads coordinated to offer Boston-to-Montreal passenger service. This included the *Mount Royal* and *Green Mountain Flyer* express trains, run until 1953, when the Rutland Railroad discontinued passenger service.

After the Boston & Maine Railroad leased the Fitchburg in 1900, the Cheshire became the Cheshire Branch of the B&M. The line had no overhead obstructions and was used for freight trains carrying high and wide loads.

Built before wide availability of concrete, construction of the line made use of skilled stone masons to carve large granite blocks that fit together perfectly without mortar. Quarries along the railroad right of way provided a convenient source of stone. The masonry bridges and piers look as solid today as they were over 150 years ago. Perhaps frost heaves are less destructive to masonry without mortar, as the rock can move without damaging the structure. The stone arch bridge just south of Keene is a particularly impressive monument to the stone mason's art.

The right of way is cut up in Keene, so the rail trails on this line are divided into the Cheshire North Trail (north of Keene) and the Cheshire South Trail (south of Keene, below Route 101). Keene is developing a bicycle route through town that will connect the three main trails: Ashuelot, Cheshire North, and Cheshire South. Nobody has yet solved the problem of crossing the extremely busy Routes 101 and 12, however.

SW3. Cheshire South Trail

State Line, Fitzwilliam, to Route 101, Keene, 20 miles
Trail condition: ★★★★ Some snowmobile trail detours around wet spots; surface is a bit rocky near the northern end. ⤴ *5 m south.*
Scenery: ★★★★★ Wetlands, Mount Monadnock views, ponds, deep rock cuts, depots, railroad masonry, and a spectacular stone arch bridge.
Permitted uses: Non-motorized travel year-round; snowmobiles, ATVs, and motorized trail bikes in winter when snow-covered.
Right of way owned by: State of New Hampshire.
Maintained by: Trails Bureau, Pathways for Keene, and Monadnock Sno-Moles.

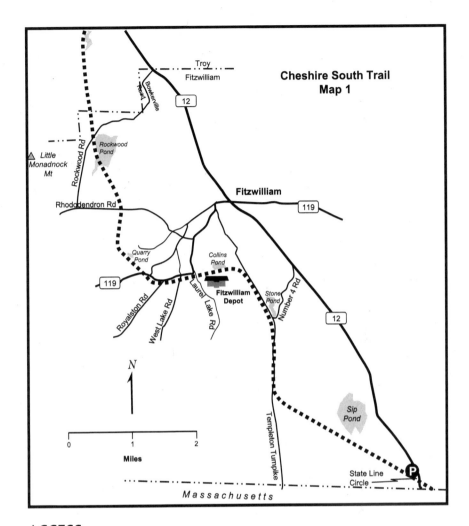

ACCESS

There is excellent access, including parking, at the southern end. A short dirt road, State Line Circle, comes off of Route 12 and affords good parking. This was the site of the State Line station.

You may be tempted to cross Route 12 and head toward Winchendon, but I recommend against it. The right of way is in terrible shape, with bad erosion, roller coasters, wet spots, and a dead end at a plastics factory. A nice wetlands view is not worth the hassle. Someday Winchendon may understand the value of rail trails, but there is no evidence of that now.

There are also many access points south and west of Fitzwilliam, permitting you to take shorter trips. However, the roads are confusing in Fitzwilliam.

Five feet of the railroad grade washed away in this spot in Massachusetts.

Given the ease of the State Line Circle access on Route 12, most long-distance users will want to start (or end) there. Access and limited parking are also available by the Troy depot and at the Swanzey Factory Road crossing.

The northern end of the trail is more problematic. There is no safe crossing of Route 101 in Keene, a very busy road. Swanzey Factory Road provides access, but it has limited parking.

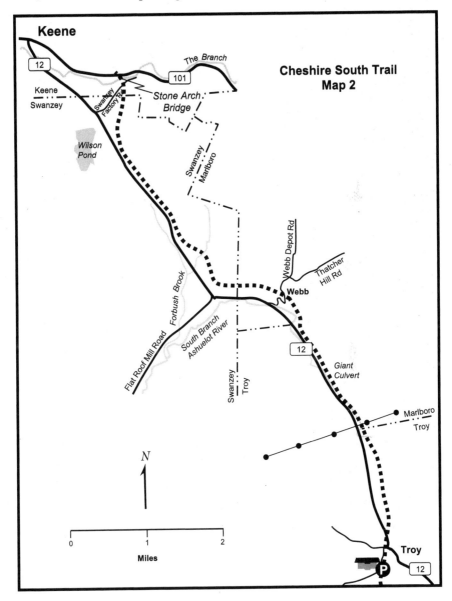

Open wetlands view near Sip Pond

DESCRIPTION

This trail offers expansive wetlands views, interesting rock cuts, and a stone arch bridge that will knock your socks off.

The Trails Bureau gates are numbered from north to south, a scheme unique to the Cheshire South Trail. For example, if you are at gate 32 near the southern end, you know you have 31 more gates to go.

Starting at the south end, you immediately obtain open views while passing over the marsh by Sip Pond. Mount Monadnock, to the northeast, is a dominant landmark. The next stretch, along Scott Brook, is woodsy, with bridges over the brook. Be sure to admire the fine craftsmanship of the stonework on the bridge supports.

In Fitzwilliam, you pass Collins Pond, Fitzwilliam Depot, and several road crossings. Just beyond Royalston Road, the railroad went through a small pass. Railroads often reduced their climbs to passes by making deep cuts at the high points, and the Cheshire made an impressive rock cut here. The railroad right of way in the cut is now poorly drained and a quagmire, so the trail diverges

This impressive stone arch bridge is the highlight of the Cheshire South Trail.

from the railroad's path. You can get a good look at the cut by taking the short "Bull Run Trail" marked with lettering carved into a trailside boulder.

A quarry pond slightly north of the Route 119 crossing appears to be a site from which the railroad obtained granite blocks for construction of bridges. Rockwood Pond, about a half mile north of Rhododendron Road, is a sizable lake. Besides being a pretty setting on its own, the lake provides enough of an opening to get another view of Mount Monadnock.

You'll know you've reached Troy when you see the remodeled Troy Depot. Now a two-story structure, it was originally one story. Nearby is the freight house, which has not been updated.

From Troy, you start making your way downstream along the South Branch of the Ashuelot River. Because the river gorge is narrow here, the trail stays close to Route 12. About a mile north of the power lines, both the highway and the railroad grade cross the river on top of a huge concrete culvert.

The descent northward along the South Branch is pleasant, if undistinguished. After the corridor leaves this drainage area, it arrives at the highlight of the trail, the magnificent stone arch bridge across a tributary of the Ashuelot called "The Branch." Built in 1848, this bridge is the largest remaining stone arch bridge in New Hampshire, and possibly in New England. It has stood proudly for over a century and a half, but currently needs some care.

The bridge over Route 101 is long gone, and there is no safe way to pass over the highway. I recommend terminating your tour by backtracking to Swanzey Factory Road after viewing the stone arch bridge. If you decide to take your chances crossing the highway, the old railroad right of way is overgrown, so you have to take Marlboro Street to the Keene Industrial Heritage Trail. This is a work in progress. Check with Pathways for Keene for up-to-date information about trail construction and recommended streets for traveling through town.

SW4. Cheshire North Trail

Wentworth Road, Westmoreland, to Ashuelot River Trail, Keene, 14 miles
Trail condition: ★ ★ ★ ★ Generally good surface with cinders and some stones; poorly drained cuts require detours.

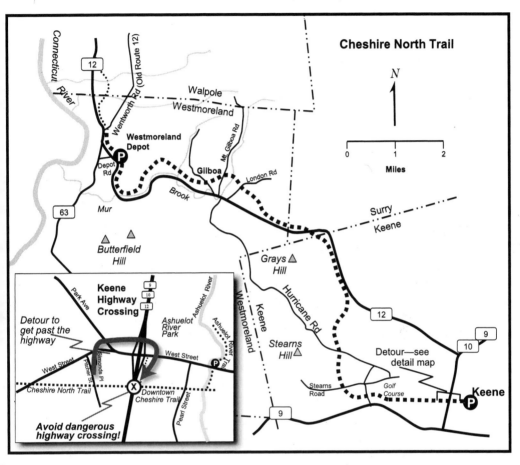

Scenery: ★★★★★ Views of hills, nicely maintained fields and farm houses, interesting automated signaling equipment, and stone masonry work; Route 12 is often close, but not intrusive.

Permitted uses: Non-motorized travel year-round; snowmobiles, ATVs, and motorized trail bikes in winter when snow-covered.

Right of way owned by: State of New Hampshire.

Maintained by: Trails Bureau, Pathways for Keene, Westmoreland Sno-Belters, and Hooper Hill Hoppers.

ACCESS

The northern end of the trail is at Old Route 12 in Westmoreland, but it is hard to spot and there is no parking. It is best to start at Depot Road, slightly to the south, where you will find decent parking. At the southern end, there is good

Scenic pastoral views from high over state Route 12.

parking just east of the Ashuelot River at the intersection of West Street and the Ashuelot River Trail. Take the West Street exit off of combined Routes 9, 10, and 12 and go east on West Street to the Ashuelot River Park.

DESCRIPTION

Most of my scouting trips have had surprises, and the Cheshire North Trail was no exception. Given that the trail is close to state Route 12 most of the way, I was expecting a dull ride. Instead, the trail turned out to have both scenic views and interesting railroad artifacts.

Various problems, such as landowner disputes, keep the railroad right of way from being a usable trail north of Old Route 12. I'll describe the trail from Old Route 12 southward, assuming you either got dropped off at Old Route 12 or came up from Depot Road.

It's hard to spot the trail at Old Route 12, as the railroad bridge is missing. The only clue is a masonry abutment for the railroad overpass. A steep path there goes up to the railroad grade from the road.

NEW HAMPSHIRE RAIL TRAILS

You pass an interesting rock cut and then come to the Depot Road parking. Nothing remains of the Westmoreland Depot except a cement slab. A billboard full of snowmobile signs reassures you that this is the trail.

A number of cuts protect the trail from nearby Route 12. Moreover, the trail soon veers away from the road and gains considerable elevation over it. When there are openings to the south, you'll obtain scenic pastoral vistas.

A deep rock cut by London Road should be a scenic part of the trail. Unfortunately, the road builders filled in the overpass for the road, blocking the railroad right of way. Once blocked, the drainage was spoiled, so the trail is a morass. A snowmobile path detours around this area. Further along the trail, you'll find that Hurricane Road has the same kind of fill blocking the trail. The lesson here: it is cheaper to replace a railroad overpass with a fill than to repair the road bridge, but the fill approach has a very high cost to the integrity of the railroad corridor!

The Route 12 bridge marks the summit of the Cheshire North Trail as it crosses from the Connecticut to the Ashuelot River valley. The railroad engineers minimized the height with a substantial rock cut that you *can* ride through, thanks to a recent effort to bring in hardpack and ditch the sides. What did the railroad construction crew do with all the rock removed from the cut? A lot of it went into an immaculate cut stone retaining wall.

View toward Butterfield Hill

US&S Automated Signaling System

Strange metal containers scattered along the Cheshire North trail puzzled me initially. Clues eventually pointed to their role as part of an early automated signaling system.

It was common in the nineteenth century for single-track lines like the Cheshire to suffer train wrecks due to misunderstandings and lack of communication among the train engineers. George Westinghouse, a pioneer inventor of railroad safety equipment, revolutionized the previously hazardous occupation of brakeman with his air brake system. He then developed a signaling system made by his company, Union Switch & Signal (US&S) of Swissdale, PA. Electric signals raised and lowered a semaphore flag, telling the train engineers when it was safe to proceed.

You can still see the wires, electrical boxes, control boxes, and circular battery supports from an early (1902) version of this system on the Cheshire North trail. Please do not remove any of these objects. They are historical artifacts that should be enjoyed by all trail users.

These odd-looking metal boxes were part of an early automated semaphore system.

After you cross under the highway bridge, the rugged scenery changes, as signaled by a beaver pond on the northeast side of the trail. Proceeding toward Keene, you pass a capped town dump, a cascading brook, views of farmhouses

Retaining wall between the rock cut and the Route 12 bridge

A beautifully crafted stone arch bridge brings the railroad grade over Stearns Road.

and fields, and the bypass around the Hurricane Road fill. At Stearns Road the railroad crosses over another monument to the stonemason's art: a stone arch overpass. It is worth climbing down to the road to get a good view of it.

The golf course of the Keene Country Club signals your approach to the greater Keene area. Note how the golf course co-exists with the railroad viaduct.

When you come to the busy combined Routes 9, 10, and 12, you should *not* try to cross it. At least one trail user died attempting to do so. Instead, backtrack to the detour shown on the Keene detail map. Take Pitcher Street north, then the jog northeast on Simonds Place, and use the West Street sidewalk. It takes you under and past the highway. Then go back south on a new trail near the northbound highway off ramp, back to the Cheshire Railroad right of way.

On this side of the highway the trail is paved and is called the "Downtown Cheshire Trail." Take it across the river and then head north on the Ashuelot River Trail to get to the second car you left by the Ashuelot River Park, if you weren't planning a round trip on this lengthy trail.

Monadnock Railroad

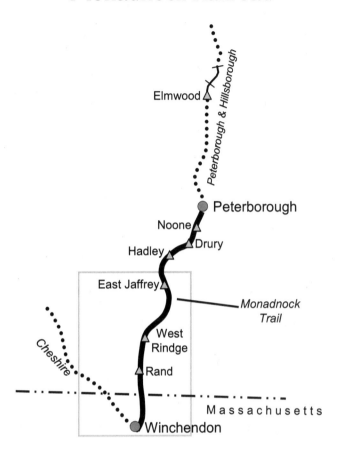

Winchendon, MA, to Peterborough
Built: 1870–71
Abandoned: 1972, 1984

The Monadnock Railroad's original charter was granted in 1848. Over twenty years later the railroad finally raised sufficient funds to build the line from Winchendon to Peterborough. It was originally a tourist line, providing passenger service for summer vacationers seeking the cool Pack Mondadnock and Grand Mònadnock mountains. The Peterborough & Hillsborough Railroad connected with it in 1878, opening the possibility of a connection with Concord.

After operating under several other railroads, the Monadnock line was taken over by the Boston & Maine in 1900. After the 1920s, cars, buses, and trucks gradually superseded the railroad in moving tourists and freight. Picturesque passenger service using old Mogul steam locomotives continued until 1953, however, and drew a large tourist trade.

The line was finally abandoned north of Jaffrey in 1972 and from Winchendon to Jaffrey in 1984. The State of New Hampshire purchased the right of way from the state line to Jaffrey in 1999 for $500,000. There is now a good trail from the state line to Jaffrey and pieces of trail leading up to Peterborough. The New Common Pathway Committee in Peterborough is attempting to complete the Jaffrey-to-Peterborough trail.

The junction of the Cheshire and Monadnock Railroads was located at Jackson Road in Winchendon. Today, both branches are overgrown near Jackson Road, and you cannot connect by trail from Winchendon to either the Monadnock Branch or Cheshire Branch trails in New Hampshire. However, you can start at Rand Road in New Hampshire and bicycle or walk south to some beautiful wetlands inside Massachusetts.

SW5. Monadnock Recreational Trail

State border, Rindge, to Hillcrest Road, Jaffrey, 7.5 miles
Trail condition: ★ ★ ★ ★ Generally good surface, frequently with cinders; some stretches in Rindge and Jaffrey are five-star.
Scenery: ★ ★ ★ ★ Views of wetlands and the headwaters of the Contoocook River.
Permitted uses: Non-motorized travel year-round; snowmobiles, ATVs, and motorized trail bikes in winter when snow-covered.
Right of way owned by: State of New Hampshire. Ownership for the Massachusetts extension is unclear, possibly private.
Maintained by: Trails Bureau and Monadnock Sno-Moles

ACCESS

At the southern end, the best access is from Route 202 at Rand Road in Rindge, about 1.7 miles north of the state line. There is room for a few cars to park at that road crossing. Rand Road is easier to find off of Route 202 than Old Danforth Road, and the latter road crossing lacks parking. There is no access from

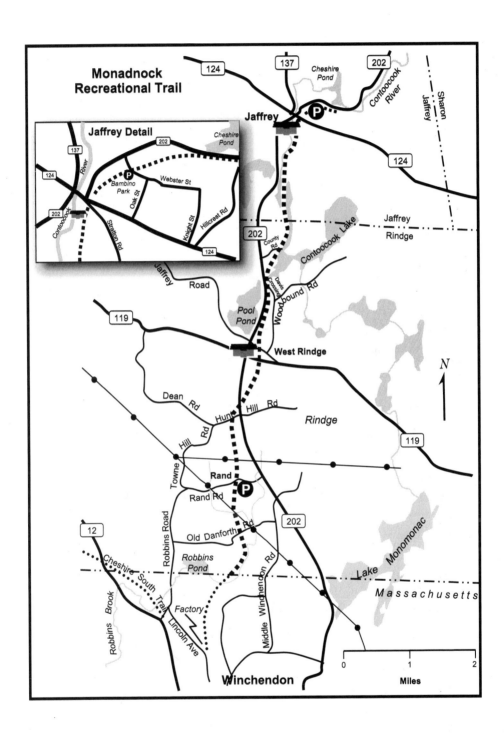

Monadnock Recreational Trail

Jaffrey Detail

This crossing near Robbins Pond was not for the faint at heart!

Winchendon, as the land by Lincoln Avenue is privately owned and posted, and the right of way is impassible south of Lincoln Avenue.

At the northern end, the best place to park is at the Bambino Park baseball field in Jaffrey. This is located on Webster Street, slightly north of the Route 202/124 intersection in the center of town.

Many other roads cross the trail, offering access and limited parking to those desiring a shorter excursion.

DESCRIPTION

This trail is a trip through scenic wetlands and lakes. Flatland views are surprising, given that the area grew up as a mountain tourist haven. The Monadnock rail line traversed a high plateau that divided the Millers River drainage to the south from the Contoocook River drainage to the north. Robbins Brook drains Robbins Pond to the south, whereas Lake Monomonac and the other lakes shown on the trail map are all part of the Contoocook headwaters.

Unlike the Cheshire line, it is well worthwhile to venture into Massachusetts on this trail. I'll start with a description of what you will see going south from old Danforth Road. This may best be accomplished with sneakers and a bathing suit. Keep in mind that I have not done research on the Massachusetts section and do not know if it is privately owned.

The trail goes along the brook that flows into Robbins Pond, affording outstanding wetland views. At the state boundary, you come across a cement marker planted in 1894. Soon thereafter, the railroad grade crosses the brook. The bridge is missing, and the brook is fairly deep. When I scouted, some precarious boards allowed passage with bicycles, but if the boards are missing, you will need to swim. More wetlands views follow, and then the trail proceeds through the woods on a cinders base. This happy situation doesn't last. Railroad ties make a poor surface for riding, and the trail peters out by a large red factory building off of Lincoln Avenue. It appears decrepit but is partially in use and is plastered with No Trespassing signs.

Returning to the "real" trail in New Hampshire, proceed north from Old Danforth Road. The trail passes through woods, crossing several roads and two power lines. Major crossings at Routes 202 and 119 are not particularly problematic, since the traffic is light in this area. Just north of the 119 crossing,

Contoocook Lake is shallow and abounds with water lilies.

you pass the West Rindge Station, now a private residence. The trail follows Route 202 closely for a while, allowing glimpses of Pool Pond across the road and through the trees.

After Davis Crossing, the trail is named the "Jack Dupre Memorial Trail" for a two-mile stretch in northern Rindge and southern Jaffrey. The trail is very nicely maintained here, with an excellent surface and park benches to rest and have lunch. Water is again the main scenery theme. After passing a wetland to the east, the trail closely follows the long arm of Contoocook Lake.

Just before reaching Route 124, you pass by the East Jaffrey depot, complete with signal semaphore still in place. This was originally a one-story building, but has been remodeled as two stories. At Route 124 you enter the hustle and bustle of downtown Jaffrey. Across the road the trail seems to end; but go another block and a paved trail starts up again. It soon passes Bambino Park, where parking is available.

At the end of the paved trail, the railroad right of way becomes problematic. It would be nice if the Jaffrey-to-Peterborough stretch were usable as a trail, but that is not the case today. Peterborough's New Common Pathway Committee is working to make this happen.

Peterborough & Shirley Railroad

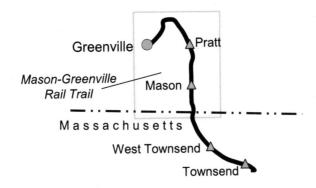

Ayer, MA, to Greenville
Built: 1848–50
Abandoned: 1979

This little railroad was another example of wishful thinking: "Build the railroad and economic prosperity will follow."

The idea was to connect the Fitchburg Railroad with Peterborough. Construction in New Hampshire reached Mason in 1850. Running out of money, the railroad managers decided they would never make it through the New Hampshire hills to Peterborough. Yet there needed to be a meaningful terminus; so they turned the line around at the northern end and went to Mason Village (now Greenville). This required a mammoth wooden bridge across the Souhegan River and Route 123, replaced later by an iron bridge.

The Peterborough & Shirley never operated as an independent entity. The Fitchburg operated it from 1850 to 1900, when the Boston & Maine took it over as their Greenville Branch. The B&M made some improvements in 1911, such as adding some additional iron trestle supports to the Souhegan bridge.

This line served several mills in Greenville and a quarry in Mason. After the textile mills closed in the 1930s, traffic was reduced. The B&M still ran freight trains from Ayer to Greenville six days a week in the 1950s, but the end was clear. After some minor storm damage in 1972, the B&M embargoed the line north of West Townsend, MA, and formally abandoned it in 1979.

Mason acquired the right of way in that town. The state of New Hampshire bought the stretch from the Mason-Wilton border to the Greenville Bridge site.

SW6. Mason–Greenville Rail Trail

State line to Greenville Bridge site, 9 miles

Trail condition: South of Pratt Pond: ★ ★ ★ ★ Generally good dirt surface, but buried railroad ties give a washboard effect for bicycles in some stretches; **North of Pratt Pond:** ★ ★ ★ Fair going, with some washouts.

Scenery: ★ ★ ★ ★ Woods and lake in a remote setting.

Permitted uses: State line to Pratt Pond Road: Non-motorized travel year-round; snowmobiles, ATVs, and motorized trail bikes in winter when snow-covered; **Pratt Pond to Greenville Bridge site:** same, except ATVs and motorized trail bikes allowed all year.

Right of way owned by: Town of Mason up to the Mason-Wilton border; state of New Hampshire northwest of the Mason-Wilton border.

Maintained by: Town of Mason up to Pratt Pond; Trails Bureau northwest of Pratt Pond.

ACCESS

The best parking spots are by the state border on Route 123 and at Pratt Pond. If you are bicycling, my recommendation is to park at the south end, ride the trail, and then return by some of the scenic back roads to get a better view of the area.

The parking spot at the state border is a turnout on the west side of Route 123, near the intersection of Morse Road. Traveling south on 123, it is about 2½ miles after the right turn 123 makes in Mason. It is easy to miss, as there is no sign marking the state border. From there the trail is a short way east on Morse Road. Coming from the south, be aware that the Route 123 designation only applies in New Hampshire. In Townsend, MA, this is Mason Road.

DESCRIPTION

This is a nice trail to bike or walk when you want to "get away from it all." The trail, like the railroad that preceded it, is unpretentious and friendly. Despite frequent road crossings, it still feels remote.

If you explore south from Morse Road, the right of way quickly deteriorates. First you hop along railroad ties still in place, then the brush hits you. Since this is a lost cause, you might as well turn around and head north.

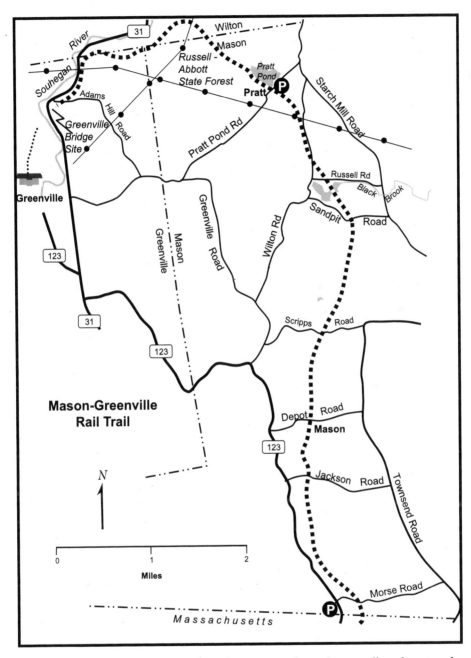

Mason-Greenville Rail Trail

N

0	1	2	

Miles

Starting north from Morse Road, you pass through a small rock cut and then cross over a dirt road, Jackson Road. The cut granite masonry on this overpass is not quite as fine as on the Cheshire trail, but the workmanship is still superior to what you'll see in later railroads.

The author by Pratt Pond. The gully here is typical of the state-owned section of trail. (Jim Sindelar)

The next road crossing is the paved Depot Road. There is a house here, and there is some controversy over whether it was the depot, heavily remodeled and moved 60 feet. It does not look like a depot.

After Scripps Road, you come to an interesting granite retaining wall beside the right of way for a spur track to the Mason Quarry (private property).

A couple of stretches of the trail feel odd to bike on, but should not cause any problem for hikers. They feel like riding on corduroy, because the railroad ties were covered up to make the trail. This is not a good idea, as the spaces between the ties inevitably compress more than the dirt on the ties, creating this ripple effect.

Soon after you pass Sandpit Road, you come to a pond on Black Brook, cut in two by the railroad grade. There is a surprisingly steep descent to a narrow bridge crossing the brook. If you are biking, watch out and get in low gear for the climb out!

You then pass Russell Road and Wilton Road on the way to Pratt Pond. The Pratt Pond road crossing appears to be where the state rules take over from the

The original Greenville Bridge, built by the Fitchburg Railroad, was a wooden covered bridge with the track on top. (Collection of Diane Karr)

The Boston & Maine Railroad replaced the wooden bridge with an iron one and added additional metal supports. (Collection of Diane Karr)

town of Mason's, so ATVs are allowed   north of there. The pond is attractive—one of many relaxing places to picnic on the trail.

Brookline & Milford provided for this extension, which was completed in 1894. Using the Pepperell-to-Milford lines and the Manchester & Milford, the Fitchburg was able to compete with the Boston & Maine Railroad for traffic from Massachusetts to Manchester and Concord. This battle was short-lived, however, as the B&M acquired the Fitchburg a few years after completion of the Brookline & Milford. This line became part of the B&M's Ayer & Milford Branch.

This little railroad had a short life. It was one of the last lines built in New Hampshire and one of the first to be abandoned. The town of Milford worked with the state of New Hampshire to buy most of the right of way in Milford. The Milford Conservation Commission made arrangements with several private landowners to complete the Granite Town Rail Trail. Brookline has continued the trail from the Milford border to Scabbard Mill Brook Road.

The Brookline Conservation Commission purchased most of the railroad right of way in Brookline from Guilford Rail System and is working to turn it into a trail. Camp Tevia owns a section at Lake Potanipo and does not allow passage when camp is in session in the summer. South of the pond, the railroad grade follows the Nissitissit River to Pepperell, MA. The Beaver Brook Association owns a couple of miles of the Potanipo Railroad Trail along the grade in Hollis and Pepperell.

SW7. Granite Town Rail Trail

South Street (Route 13), Milford, to Scabbard Mill Brook Road, Brookline, 6 miles (Note: The name "Granite Town Rail Trail" officially applies only to the part of the trail in Milford.)

Trail condition: ★★★ Tree roots across the trail make this primarily a hiking path.

Scenery: ★★★★★ Woods, ponds, and brooks in a rustic setting.

Permitted uses: Non-motorized travel; best for walking. A short stretch through the Palmer Preserve in Brookline is labeled "No Wheeled Vehicles," but I was told by the Brookline Conservation Commission that bicycles are permitted.

Right of way owned by: Town of Milford, with some easements over private property in Milford; Town of Brookline and Palmer Wildlife Preserve in Brookline.

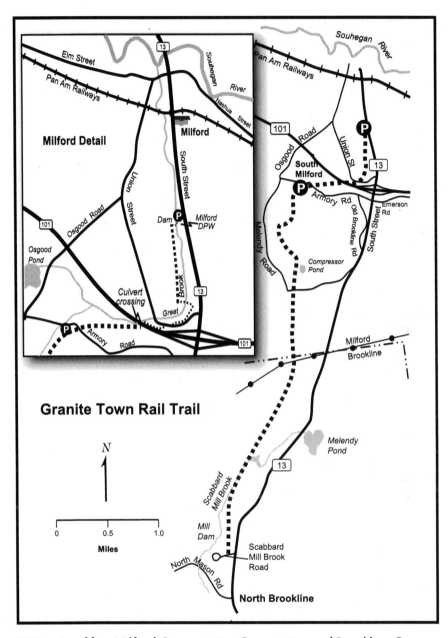

Milford Detail

Milford

Granite Town Rail Trail

N

| 0 | 0.5 | 1.0 |

Miles

North Brookline

Maintained by: Milford Conservation Commission and Brookline Conservation Commission

The small parking area off Armory Road is unusually attractive, with a stone retaining wall. This may have been the location of the South Milford Station.

ACCESS

The northern access to the trail is at the Milford Department of Public Works at 283 South Street. Park to the right of the DPW buildings, walk behind the fence, and cross Great Brook on an old dam to get to the trail (see Milford Detail map). Sometimes this portion of the trail gets flooded by beavers. In that case, use a charming parking area on Armory Road, about three-fourths mile west of Route 13 in Milford. Melendy Road, near the trail's midpoint, and Scabbard Mill Brook Road at the southern end provide trail access but no parking.

DESCRIPTION

This trail is ideal for a pleasant stroll through the woods. The large pine trees show that the railroad has been gone for the better part of a century. Their shallow roots across the trail make slow, bumpy going for mountain bikes.

Starting at the northern parking area on South Street, a narrow trail goes behind the DPW building and crosses the brook on a small dam to get to the railroad grade. For a short distance, the trail goes through woods on the railroad right of way, but then takes a narrow path around and through an area that often floods from beaver activity.

South of the beaver-threatened stretch, the trail wanders around wetlands, crosses Union Street, and traverses the bottom of the Route 101 embankment to an odd culvert. It is unclear whether the culvert was designed to allow severe floodwaters to pass under Route 101, act as a wildlife crossing, or allow fishermen and snowmobiles to cross. In any case, it provides a handy below-grade crossing of the highway. The opening appears to be too small, but you can make it through.

Once you get south of 101, the trail really begins. Continuing west to the Armory Road parking area, you get an initial taste for the narrow, tree-lined trail.

South of Armory Road, there is a diversion up a hill to avoid a trailer park that took over part of the original railroad grade. After returning to the railroad right of way, you pass Compressor Pond, the first of three ponds you will see.

Culvert under Route 101

The trail winds through the pine trees and is bumpy from their roots.

The railroad underpass at Melendy Road has been filled, requiring a climb up to the road and down again. In early November 2006, I saw a trail biker returning from a short jaunt on the south side of Melendy Road, the one section of the trail where off-road vehicles are allowed.

Soon you come to the Brookline town line, where signs indicate that motorized vehicles have to turn around. The trail is quite scenic the rest of the way, with a rustic trail surface, a couple of ponds, and Scabbard Mill Brook. The mill dam is worth a look.

After crossing a driveway, the trail ends somewhat abruptly at Scabbard Mill Brook Road.

SW8. Potanipo Railroad Trail

Oak Hill Road, Brookline, to Prescott Street, Pepperell, MA, 3 miles (interrupted by the Nissitissit River).
Trail condition: ★ ★ ★ Missing bridge and culvert, tree roots, and rocks in Brookline. The trail is much easier going east of Pepperell Road, but tree roots make it rough for bicyclists.

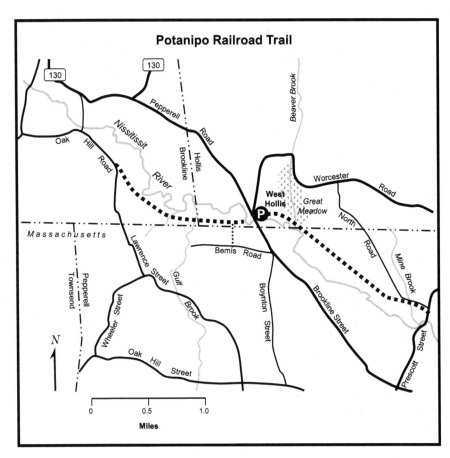

Potanipo Railroad Trail

Scenery: ★★★★ Views of Great Meadow are worth the trip.

Permitted uses: Non-motorized travel; best for walking. Horses are not allowed east of Pepperell Road, but bicycles are permitted.

Right of way owned by: Beaver Brook Association and Nissitissit River Land Trust in New Hampshire; Massachusetts Fish & Game in Massachusetts.

Maintained by: Beaver Brook Association.

ACCESS

There is a large parking area in West Hollis on the east side of Pepperell Road, just north of the state line and the Nissitissit River road bridge. Only the abutments remain of the Nissitissit River railroad bridge, so the trail has two disjointed sections. To reach the western section, take Bemis Road in Pepperell to a path that heads north to the trail. On the west end, a very narrow path from Oak Hill Road goes around a white house to reach the trail. It is so hidden that you should use the Bemis Road approach. The eastern section starts at the West Hollis parking area.

DESCRIPTION

Western section (1.3 miles): After taking the path from Bemis Road to the rail trail, take a short side trip east to see the Nissitissit River bridge site. The abutments are in good shape, but the bridge is long gone. You get nice views of the narrow, meandering Nissitissit both upstream and downstream.

Turning back west, there is a missing bridge across Gulf Brook, requiring a climb down to a beaver dam and back up. About one-fifth mile further west, an eroded culvert requires a similar scramble. ATV and snowmobile users find ways around these obstacles, although the Beaver Brook Association discourages motorized vehicles on the trail. The scenery is mostly piney woods.

Eastern section (1.8 miles): Shortly after leaving the parking lot, the trail passes the south end of Great Meadow, a large wetland area. The footbridge

The washed out culvert in Brookline requires a scramble.

NEW HAMPSHIRE RAIL TRAILS

View of Great Meadow from the Beaver Brook foot bridge. Note the culvert and wire cage mechanism to prevent the beavers from flooding the trail.

across Beaver Brook is a hazard for horses and is the reason they are not allowed on this section of the trail.

Past Great Meadow, the trail offers a relaxed stroll through the pine trees. Toward the end it closely follows North Road to the intersection of Prescott Street, where there is a former one-room schoolhouse that has been converted to a home. Although the right of way continues southeast of Prescott Street, it is heavily overgrown and is missing a bridge.

Manchester & Keene Railroad

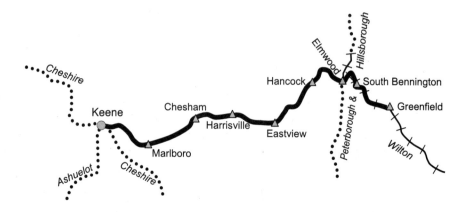

Greenfield to Keene
Built: 1875–78
Abandoned: Keene–Elmwood, 1938–39

When you look at a map of southwestern New Hampshire, it seems natural that someone would try to connect Keene with the Concord Railroad at either Manchester or Nashua. But if you've ever driven west toward Keene on either Route 101 or Route 9, you realize how difficult it would be to construct a level route through this hilly country.

Efforts to build the Manchester & Keene Railroad required substantial capital, both stock purchased by railroad shareholders and assessments on the towns served, called gratuities. Construction began in 1875 and was plagued by financial difficulties. Railroad owners went broke, contractors weren't paid and went under, and laborers and the townspeople who lodged them were unpaid. Yet somehow the line was built.

Given the extraordinarily difficult terrain and chronic financial shortfalls, the M&K did not reach Greenfield until 1878, just after the Peterborough & Hillsborough line reached the junction at Elmwood.

With little revenue base, the M&K was never a financial success. The acquisitive Boston & Maine Railroad kept running trains on the line (calling it the Nashua & Keene Branch) until January 1934. At that time a new fill, which replaced Rice's Trestle east of Hancock, gave way. Since there were few paying customers west of there, the B&M discontinued service on that part of the line and abandoned it a few years later. Freight service continued east of Rice's

The bridges, cuts, and fills on the Manchester & Keene Railroad were impressive. Top: Alcock wooden trestle. Bottom: Newell Trestle in operation and as it appears today. (Historical photos courtesy of the Hancock Historical Society)

Trestle to Elmwood until the great hurricane of 1938. That storm caused more bridge damage, and the line was totally abandoned except for the segment from Elmwood to Greenfield.

All of the bridges are gone now, making for a chopped up railroad right of way. However, there are some privately owned stretches where the right of way is in good shape. The town of Harrisville is working on opening up some trail east of Lake Skatutakee. Hancock has a short stretch open to the public from the Hancock depot to a missing bridge over Moose Brook. A tour route through these towns, comprising both rail trail and road stretches, would provide great access to the excellent scenery of this area. Some trail planning is also going on in Marlborough. I strongly encourage readers to get involved in these efforts.

Peterborough & Hillsborough Railroad

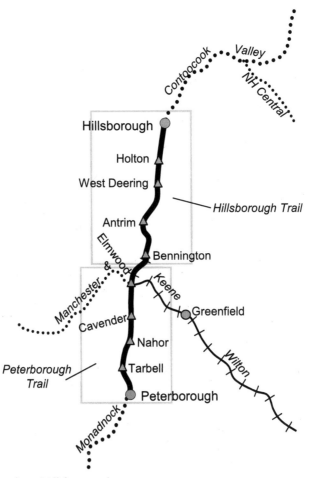

Peterborough to Hillsborough
Built: 1877–78
Abandoned: Peterborough–Elmwood, 1942; Bennington–Hillsborough, 1979

The Contoocook Valley Railroad had reached Hillsborough by 1849, where it came to a dead end. The Peterborough & Shirley attempted to reach Peterborough in the late 1840s, but ran out of money and terminated at Greenville. The Civil War and post-war depression caused a lull in railroad construction. Then came a period of feverish railroad building in the boom period of the 1870s in the Peterborough–Hillsborough part of the state. The Monadnock Railroad reached Peterborough in 1871. The Wilton line (then called the Nashua & Lowell) reached Greenfield in 1874. The Manchester & Keene connected with it in 1878, the same year that the Peterborough & Hillsborough line was completed.

The Boston, Barre & Gardner Railroad undertook construction of the P&H after they leased the Monadnock line. Clearly a connection with the Contoocook Valley would enable through service that would make the Monadnock Railroad more profitable. Funds were tight, however, and construction did not begin until the Northern Railroad agreed to lease the line. The Boston & Lowell took over operations from 1884 to 1887, and the sprawling Boston & Maine took over the P&H in 1888 as part of its Worcester & Hillsborough Branch.

After steady operations through the First World War and the 1920s, the inevitable automobile-induced decline set in. When a storm damaged part of the rail bed in 1936, the B&M discontinued all passenger service on the line, as well as freight service from Peterborough to Elmwood. It abandoned the Hillsborough-to-Bennington line much later, in 1979. The short stretch from Elmwood to Bennington still has state-owned track in place intended to serve the Monadnock Paper Mills plant, but no railroad has stepped up to provide that service.

After abandonment, the Peterborough-to-Elmwood section was cut up into privately owned sections. However, the New Common Pathway Committee in Peterborough has done a marvelous job of creating a trail on this stretch. Abandoned much later, the Hillsborough-to-Bennington stretch was bought by the state of New Hampshire and became the Hillsborough Recreational Trail.

Elmwood Junction, 1904. The train at right is a passenger train from Keene to Nashua. The train at left is a passenger train from Winchendon to Concord. (Courtesy of the Hancock Historical Society)

SW9. Peterborough Trail (The Old Railroad Trail)

Summer Street, Peterborough, to South Elmwood Road, Hancock, 9 miles

Trail condition: ★ ★ ★ ★ Surface varies from dirt to pavement to stretches of paved road; generally very easy riding.

Scenery: ★ ★ ★ ★ Woods, Contoocook River, ponds; varies from remote to suburban settings.

Permitted uses: Non-motorized travel plus snowmobiles in winter north of Route 202. ATVs and motorized trail bikes are definitely not allowed. The private landowners get particularly upset by OHRVs.

Right of way owned by: Private parties in Hancock; mostly owned by the town in Peterborough.

Maintained by: Peterborough's New Common Pathway Committee (Conservation Commission) and Monadnock Trail Breakers.

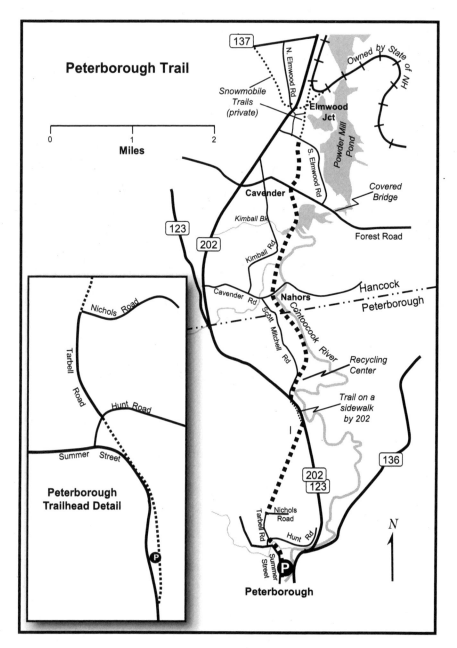

Peterborough Trail

0   1   2
Miles

137

Snowmobile
Trails
(private)

N. Elmwood Rd

Owned by State of NH

**Elmwood
Jct**

S. Elmwood Rd

Powder Mill
Pond

Cavender

Kimball Bk

Covered
Bridge

123

202

Kimball Rd

Forest Road

Cavender Rd

Nahors

Scott Mitchell Rd

Contoocook River

Hancock
Peterborough

Recycling
Center

Trail on a
sidewalk
by 202

202
123

136

Nichols
Road

Tarbell Rd

Hunt Rd

Summer
Street

P

Peterborough

N

Peterborough Trailhead Detail

Nichols Road

Tarbell Road

Hunt Road

Summer Street

P

ACCESS

Trail parking at the southern end is on Summer Street, about a mile north of Main Street in downtown Peterborough. Summer Street is just west of the

Mile marker by a Contoocook River view, a few hundred yards north of Cavender Road

stone arch bridge where Main Street crosses the Contoocook River. The parking area is about one-tenth mile north of the trail start on Summer Street (see detail map). At the northern end, there is a turnout where the trail crosses Forest Road. Going east on Forest Road from Route 202, if you come to the covered bridge, you've overshot the trail. In the middle, you can park near the Peterborough recycling center off Scott Mitchell Road near Route 202.

DESCRIPTION

This trail is definitely worth exploring for its diversity of scenery on an easy ride. The Hancock stretch is a typical rural rail trail with some pond and river scenes. The Peterborough stretch is more densely settled but still has enjoyable farmland, well kept houses, and water scenery. Peterborough's New Common Pathway Committee deserves a lot of credit for creating a trail out of a right of way chopped up by multiple roads. They even managed to get a culvert passage under the section taken over by a US Route 202 rerouting.

Here's what you'll see as you go north from the Summer Street trailhead:

From the parking lot, proceed on a paved path by a lagoon near the Contoocook River. This leads to a short stretch on Tarbell Road, which was built on the railroad right of way. That brings you to an immaculate paved trail through the woods to Route 202.

After passing the driveway to Southfield Village (an apartment complex), you come to the stretch of Route 202 that took over the railroad bed. The New Common Pathway Committee created a paved sidewalk for trail users on the west side of 202 up to the culvert underpass.

The trail surface changes to smooth gravel as the trail passes the Peterborough recycling center. Since the trail snuggles up to the Contoocook River here, you get attractive views of the river. The surface quality declines as you go further north, with some roots across the trail, but it is still quite easy to walk or ride on.

The views change to pristine farmland as you near the Hancock town line. There is a particularly scenic farm field and house on the Contoocook floodplain after you pass Cavender Road (dirt). Next is a handsome antique brick farmhouse.

You get another view of the river as it bends against the trail at the 57/14 mile marker, one of the railroad's cement mile markers on the trail. From there the trail veers away from the river and floodplain farms and heads into the woods. You get pond views as you cross over the cement culvert for Kimball Brook.

Forest Road is the northern trailhead as far as parking goes, but you can continue through the woods to South Elmwood Road. This is all private property, so be respectful, especially in obeying the motorized vehicle prohibition.

SW10. Hillsborough Recreational Trail

Bennington Depot, Bennington, to Union Street, Hillsborough, 8 miles
Trail condition: ★ ★ ★ ★ Some wet spots; ties and rails at the south end; sandy by the landing strip.
Scenery: ★ ★ ★ ★ Farmland, Contoocook River, settled areas.
Permitted uses: Non-motorized travel plus ATVs, motorized trail bikes, and snowmobiles (year-round use of OHRVs).
Right of way owned by: State of New Hampshire.
Maintained by: Trails Bureau and Tri County OHRV Club.

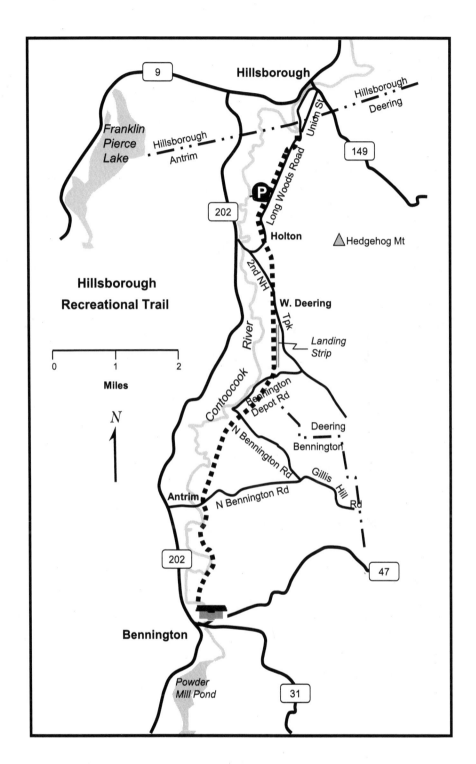

Hillsborough Recreational Trail

Miles
0 1 2

N

The Hillsborough trail offers picturesque farm scenery.

ACCESS

At the northern end, the Trails Bureau has arranged for trail parking at the Deering Fish & Game Club on Long Woods Road, about 2 miles south of Route 149. To get to the southern end, go east on Routes 47 and 31 from Route 202. You come immediately to the old Bennington depot, now VFW Post 8268, which is the trailhead. Although the VFW has posted No Unauthorized Parking signs, you may be able to park a car close to the depot.

DESCRIPTION

This is a pleasant if unspectacular trail that is so convenient, with easy access off Route 202, that it begs to be seen.

Heading south along Long Woods Road, there is a view of Hedgehog Mountain to the East. Then you cross the Second New Hampshire Turnpike and start seeing the farms that characterize this region.

The trail passes close to the Hawthorne-Feather Airpark landing strip in Antrim. It is still in active use but looks as if maintenance has been deferred. The trail is quite sandy by the landing strip.

Shortly after the airpark, the trail crosses Bennington Depot Road. The name is puzzling, as the road is now disconnected from the depot. Pleasant farm scenery continues. North Bennington Road crosses twice; the second crossing was the location of the Antrim depot.

At cement mile marker W62, the trail passes alongside railroad ties and becomes rail with trail. This is the rail line from Wilton that the state owns, and you will see the spur track leading to the Monadnock Paper Mills plant. The paper company would like train service, and the state upgraded the track to allow it; but apparently the economics still favor truck transportation.

Just north of the Bennington depot, a bridge over the Contoocook River offers a view of a rapid that looks perfect for whitewater kayaking. The bridge has an unusual heavy rubber mat over the ties that acts as decking to walk on.

The trail ends at the Bennington depot, now a local VFW.

New Boston Railroad

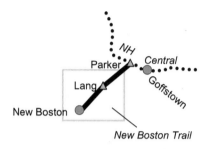

New Boston to Goffstown
Built: 1893
Abandoned: 1935

The New Boston Railroad was created to transport fresh farm products to J. Reed Whipple's three hotels in Boston. It connected with the New Hampshire Central (then under the control of the Concord & Montreal Railroad) near Goffstown and was intended to continue on to Milford. It never got any further than New Boston. The elaborate depot there, designed by famous architect Bradford Lee Gilbert, burned down in 1895. Gilbert designed another even more lavish depot replacement. It is an example of how even a tiny, rural railroad competed to be modern and stylish in the nineteenth century.

The wood, stucco, and stone New Boston depot is now a private residence.

The railroad was abandoned in 1935. New Boston gained ownership of most of the right of way from the 4H County Fairgrounds to Route 114. It is now a fine walking trail by the South Branch of the Piscataquog River.

SW11. New Boston Rail Trail

New Boston Depot to Route 114, 5 miles
Trail condition: ★ ★ ★ Some wet spots and tree roots; narrow trail best for walking; first mile to 4H Fairgrounds is dirt road.
Scenery: ★ ★ ★ ★ South Branch Piscataquog River.
Permitted uses: Non-motorized travel only.

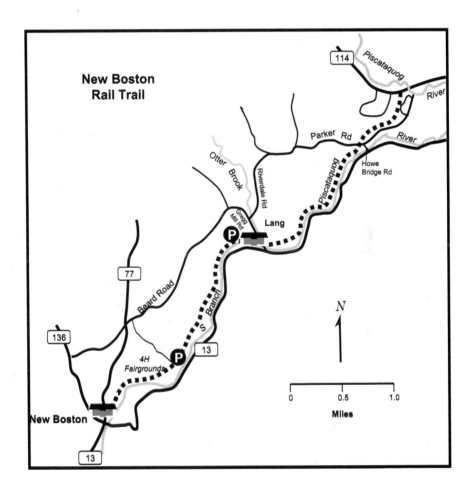

A narrow path by the South Branch Piscataquog River

Right of way owned by: Town of New Boston and New Hampshire Conservation Land Investment Program; a short stretch by Parker Road is privately owned.
Maintained by: Town of New Boston.

ACCESS

I recommend starting at the south end of this trail in the center of New Boston, where Routes 136, 77, and 13 all meet. A quaint firehouse is on the east side of the river, and the depot is on the west side. The town recommends parking either at the 4H Fairgrounds or at Lang Station on Gregg Mill Road, but you can also park in the town center and go from there. Route 13 is on the east side of the river, and you can cross on either Gregg Mill Road or Howe Bridge Road to reach the trail on the west side. No parking is available at the northern end where the trail meets Route 114.

DESCRIPTION

New Boston did a fine job of acquiring much of the railroad right of way and working with private landowners to make this trail a reality.

Like the Granite Town Rail Trail in Milford, this is more of a hiking trail than a bike path. It is very narrow in spots and goes between mature pine trees with roots on the trail. Motorized vehicles are prohibited in all seasons, so the trail is peaceful. It follows the South Branch of the Piscataquog River, whose gentle rapids are visible most of the way.

Starting at New Boston Depot on the south end, the first mile is a dirt road into the 4H County Fairgrounds. New Boston's trail starts there, and you will notice a big difference between the wide road leading in and the narrow path going out toward Goffstown. In places, the trail is only a couple of feet wide between trees, and tree roots often cover it. The river is always close by to the south.

Lang Station is a simple stone shelter.

At Gregg Mill Road you come to the stone shelter that was Lang Station and a parking area. The town's new foot bridge over Otter Brook allows you to continue to Goffstown. The right of way goes through some house lots near Parker Road, requiring a bit of a detour over private property around houses and a climb over Parker Road. The trail comes to a dead end at Route 114.

New Hampshire Central Railroad

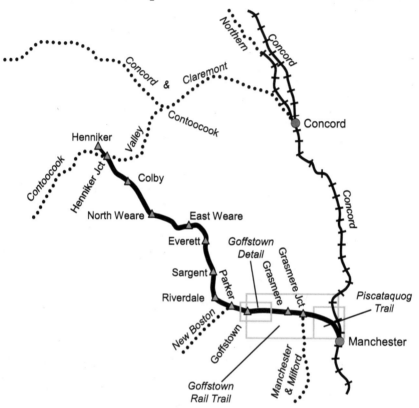

Manchester to Henniker Junction
Built: 1850
Abandoned: Goffstown-Henniker Junction, 1937; Manchester-Goffstown, 1981

This railroad was an early one, built in 1849-50, with the intention of linking Manchester with Claremont. Since the area it went through was mostly farming communities, revenue was slight and the railroad only made it to Henniker, where it met the Contoocook Valley Railroad (completed in 1849). The hope was to use the Contoocook Valley to reach Contoocook and the Concord & Claremont Railroad to finally reach Claremont. As originally constructed, the railroad went past Henniker Junction, crossed the Contoocook River, and ended at a depot in downtown Henniker.

Money ran out, and the New Hampshire Central fell into the hands of the Concord Railroad in 1858. The Concord insisted on tearing up the track from

Henniker Junction in 1933. The gas-electric train at left is going to Concord. B&M #1019 at right is coming from Manchester. (William Monypeny photo from the collection of Brent S. Michiels)

North Weare to Henniker to avoid competition with their Manchester-to-Concord main line. The Concord and the Boston, Concord & Montreal joined forces in 1889, forming the Concord & Montreal Railroad. The new railroad restored the North Weare-to-Henniker Junction link but made no attempt to recreate the link from Henniker Junction to downtown Henniker.

Transporting agricultural supplies and produce was never particularly lucrative, even after the Boston & Maine acquired the line in 1895. With the inevitable railroad decline in the early twentieth century, the line was finally abandoned from Goffstown to Henniker Junction in 1937 and from Manchester to Goffstown in 1981.

Land sales and development leave little hope for trails on a line abandoned 70 years ago. Route 114 took the right of way from Henniker Junction to Colby. The most intact section north of Goffstown is clearly posted No Trespassing. However, the more recently abandoned section is now the subject of active trail creation projects in Goffstown and Manchester. Also, some of the right of way from Henniker Junction to Henniker is traceable, as described under Trail SW15.

SW12. Goffstown Rail Trail

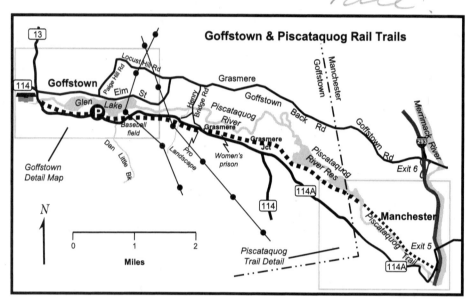

Covered railroad bridge site, Goffstown, to Piscataquog railroad bridge, Manchester, 6.5 miles

Trail condition: ★★★ Informal trail suitable for hiking, with gullies, missing bridges, wet spots, and places where it is hard to find the trail. Most of it is easy going for mountain bikes as well, and it will be upgraded.

Scenery: ★★★ Nice river and woods views, but an ugly stretch by Route 114; rating may increase to four stars after trail improvements.

Permitted uses: Non-motorized travel only; horses not allowed.

Right of way owned by: Town of Goffstown; the city of Manchester owns a short stretch within the city limits.

Maintained by: Town of Goffstown and the Friends of the Greenway.

ACCESS

Route 114 is close to the first half of the trail, but parking is hard to find. The best place to park near the western end is the Goffstown Parks & Recreation site just east of Shirley Park Road (see the Goffstown Detail map). Access to the eastern end is less obvious. It is described in the access notes for the Piscataquog Trail (SW13), the extension of the Goffstown Rail Trail into Manchester.

DESCRIPTION

This is an excellent example of an abandoned railroad corridor in a fairly densely populated area that will one day make a prime greenway (linear park). After giving up on this line, Guilford Rail System (now Pan Am Railways) kept title to the corridor. The town of Goffstown started planning in 1993 to make it a trail. Using a Transportation Enhancement grant, the town acquired the right of way from Guilford in 1998. Now the Goffstown Rail Trail Steering Committee and Friends of the Greenway are working on improving it. The trail has problems, but it is usable now.

As of 2007, Goffstown had three trail-related efforts underway. One was a survey to determine the precise ownership of each part of the trail. This will clarify how encroachments on the corridor should be handled. A second effort was "first mile" trail improvement using a state Recreational Trails Program grant. To keep costs down, the improved trail will be hardpack rather than paved. The third effort was corridor landscaping by Pro Landscape Supply to improve trail passage by their site on Mast Road (Route 114).

Here's what the trail looks like before improvements, going from west to east:

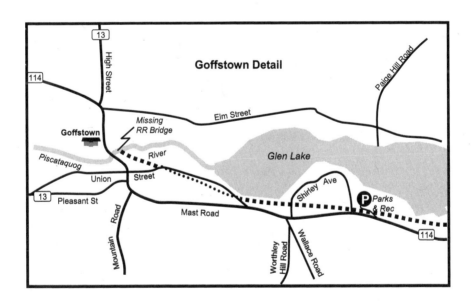

The Goffstown covered bridge stood proudly when this picture was taken in 1974. (Ron Karr)

In the center of Goffstown, you can see the depot, now used as an annex for the local Ace Hardware store. Near there, the railroad crossed the Piscataquog River on a rare covered railroad bridge. Unfortunately, an arsonist burned down this 100-foot bridge in 1976, so nothing remains but the masonry piers. The Friends of the Greenway would like to build a foot bridge using these piers to connect the trail to the center of town.

Private development had closed the railroad right of way for public use between the two Union Street crossings (see the Goffstown Detail map). Fortunately, Union Street has little traffic and is a convenient connector between trail segments. East of Union Street, the trail goes behind some houses and through trees, with an occasional view of Glen Lake to the north. The railroad bridge over a small brook is missing, so you have to scramble down, cross the brook on some rocks, and scramble up again. You may want to start at the

Goffstown Parks & Recreation facility and go east to avoid this stretch until the Friends of the Greenway have fixed it up.

Beyond the Parks & Rec site, the trail proceeds pleasantly away from the highway for a bit. When I scouted this trail, there was extensive erosion at Dan Little Brook from the Mother's Day Flood of 2006. The masonry culvert suffered some damage, and the water carved out a great deal of the sand to the side of the culvert. On the lake side, you may see the sandbar that resulted when the sandy water blasted through the culvert. The Goffstown Public Works department plans to repair the culvert and eroded hillside using FEMA funding.

After crossing the brook, you cross Route 114 (Mast Road) at a baseball field and go under the first of two sets of power lines. The mile from the baseball field east is the least interesting section of the trail, as it follows Mast Road closely. It also has a tendency to collect pools of water on the surface. The 2007 RTP grant will attack both problems for a mile east of Parks & Rec by adding landscaping to de-emphasize the highway and applying hardpack to improve the surface.

The Goffstown rail trail features water views like this one of Glen Lake.

The bridge over the old Henry's Bridge Road is missing, requiring a difficult scramble if you insist on going this way.

Further on, a Shell service station blocks the path. Eventually Goffstown will route the trail behind the Shell station on an easement. For now, take the Mast Road shoulder to bypass this obstacle.

The Manchester Street Railway ran a trolley line from Manchester to Goffstown starting in 1871. In Goffstown its path was parallel to the railroad's and close beside it on the south side. You can catch glimpses of its right of way. As

NEW HAMPSHIRE RAIL TRAILS

The trail is perched high over the reservoir (left side).

you pass the second set of power lines, the railroad corridor is blocked by two houses. The trail goes off on the trolley right of way to get around them.

The railroad corridor crosses the highway again at the eastern end of the Pro Landscape Supply facility. Do not cross Route 114 where the railroad did! This grade-level crossing is extremely dangerous due to heavy traffic and poor visibility. The recommended approach is to follow the Mast Road shoulder to Henry Bridge Road and cross over at the traffic light there. This small detour also avoids a steep gully where the railroad crossed a bridge over the old route of Henry Bridge Road. The bridge is gone, and trying to pass through the gully entails trespassing over private property.

Past the New Hampshire Women's Prison, the trail diverges from Mast Road and the scenery improves. The trail is confusing to follow at the Morgan Circle Estates condominium complex. The condominium back yard uses the railroad corridor, and beyond their buildings it takes some searching to find the trail again.

The next stretch up to and alongside the Piscataquog River Reservoir is especially scenic and easy for mountain bike riding. You go through a small rock cut and then ride through woods along the southern end of the lake, with a steep drop-off toward the water.

Shortly after crossing the Manchester city line, you come to the end of the reservoir and the railroad bridge over the river. The bridge appears to be solid, but it is not decked. For safety reasons, it is fenced off at both ends. There is no real trailhead at this end. You can backtrack or follow a paved road past a condominium complex to proceed onto the Piscataquog Trail (SW13).

SW13. Piscataquog Trail

Piscataquog River Reservoir railroad bridge to the Hands Across the Merrimack Bridge, Manchester, 1.5 miles.

Trail condition: ★★★ Surface actually varies from 1 to 5 stars; planned trail development will provide a dramatic upgrade.

Scenery: ★★★ Dramatic contrasts; first stretch has views of the Pisquataquog River; second stretch is unbelievably ugly; third section is a paved and landscaped urban greenway. Trail improvements will help.

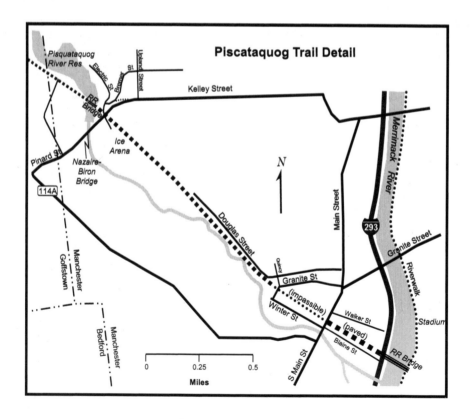

The Nazaire-Biron Bridge gives this view of the reservoir dam (foreground) and railroad bridge (background).

Permitted uses: Reservoir to Granite Street: unknown; Granite Street to South Main Street: impassible; South Main to Merrimack River bridge: non-motorized travel.
Right of way owned by: City of Manchester.
Maintained by: Manchester Parks & Recreation.

ACCESS

Walking or riding from the Goffstown Rail Trail, take the paved road that goes past a condominium complex and the sports fields in the John C. Sarette Recreation Complex near the Goffstown-Manchester border. It has a gate near the top, but the gate is usually open. Turn left onto the Pinard Street sidewalk and cross the impressive Nazaire-Biron Bridge. This becomes Kelley Street on

As of 2007, the corridor between Granite and Main Streets was an uninviting bog, but the city will upgrade it to a paved and landscaped trail.

the other side of the river. A paved footpath leads down from Kelley Street to Bremer Street. Take Bremer to Electric Street and the trail.

If you are driving, take Kelley Street to Upland Street. From Upland, turn left onto Bremer, then left again onto Electric, and park near the ice arena. At the eastern end, park on Winter Street or Blaine Street off of Main Street.

DESCRIPTION

Manchester Parks & Recreation is working on a multi-phase project to make a mile-and-a-half corridor into a paved trail that will link with the Goffstown Rail Trail to the west and the Manchester-to-Salem corridor to the east, via the Hands Across the Merrimack Bridge. Going from west to east, here is what exists now:

Cyclone fencing and No Trespassing signs block the railroad bridge over the eastern end of the Piscataquog River Reservoir. Manchester's trail improve-

The paved trail is a delightful contrast to the bog stretch. It includes grassy shoulders and decorative night lighting.

ment project will deck the bridge for pedestrian passage. From the eastern end of the bridge, the trail has a good riding surface and views of the river until Granite Street.

At that point, the corridor becomes a bog filled with trash. Don't try to go through it until this section of trail has been improved! Backtrack to Douglas Street. Go one block east and take a right on Quincy Street, another right on Granite, and then a left on Winter. Take Winter Street to South Main, and go north a half block to the start of the paved trail.

The paved trail dead-ends at the railroad bridge over the Merrimack River. You won't be surprised to see another cyclone fence and No Trespassing signs keeping people off this undecked bridge. Manchester's Hands Across the Merrimack project will turn this bridge into an attractive pedestrian bridge that connects the Goffstown and Piscataquog trails with the Manchester-to-Salem rail trails and the Riverwalk on the east side of the Merrimack. Construction work on the pedestrian bridge started in 2007.

Contoocook Valley Railroad

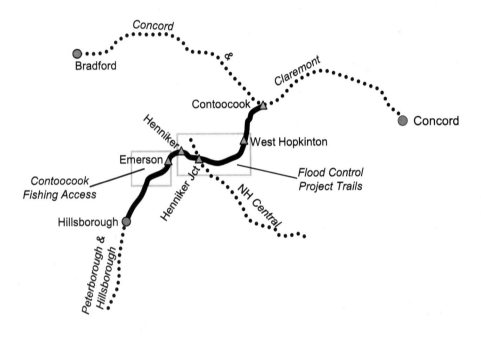

Contoocook to Hillsborough
Built: 1849
Abandoned: Hillsborough-Emerson, 1942; Emerson-West Hopkinton, 1960; West Hopkinton-Contoocook, 1961

This small connector line was one of the early railroads. Built in 1849, it provided transportation for the communities of Hillsborough and Henniker to Concord and Manchester. The Concord connection was at Contoocook, where the Concord & Claremont Railroad proceeded into Concord to the east and Bradford to the west. Much later, the C&C reached the Connecticut River at Claremont. The Manchester connection was at Henniker Junction with the New Hampshire Central Railroad.

Four and a half miles between Hillsborough and Emerson were abandoned in 1942. After serious flooding of the Contoocook River in 1958, the rest of the Contoocook Valley track was abandoned. The Army Corps of Engineers then built the massive Hopkinton-Everett Lake flood control project, which blocked the right of way.

Much of the right of way has gone to private landowners. Some interesting sections are preserved as part of the flood control project. Three short trail sections are worth investigating.

SW14. Contoocook Fishing Access

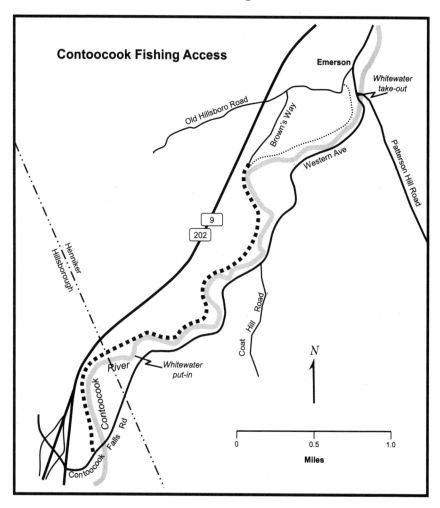

Contoocook Falls Road, Hillsborough, to Brown's Way, Henniker, 2.4 miles
Trail condition: ★★★ A dirt road providing Contoocook River fishing access. Some sections are rocky or rutted and wet.

At the southern end of the trail, the river is a calm pool.

Scenery: ★ ★ ★ ★ River rapids on one of New England's finest stretches of whitewater for decked canoes and kayaks.

Permitted uses: Unrestricted, but the roadway is rough.

Right of way owned by: Privately owned but currently used as a public road.

Maintained by: Possibly New Hampshire Fish & Game.

ACCESS

For the northern end, take Old Hillsboro Road off of Western Avenue shortly above the river crossing. Turn left on a dirt road about a fifth of a mile east of the overpass over Routes 202 and 9. This road is shown as Brown's Way on maps, but there is no sign. Brown's Way becomes the trail. The southern end is off Contoocook Falls Road (Western Avenue in Hillsborough) just southwest of the bridge across the river. Parking is very limited near both ends.

The town of Henniker refused to take ownership and responsibility for this road; there is a possibility that owners could deny access to the public.

DESCRIPTION

Nelson Maine gave a fifty-foot easement on the north side of this stretch of river to the state of New Hampshire for fishing access. This is close to and sometimes includes parts of the railroad grade, now a dirt road. The road has houses on it, and many people drive their pickups on it to go fishing, but it is rough for an automobile. Currently it is open to the public and tends to be quiet, since through traffic uses Western Avenue/Contoocook Falls Road on the other side of the river.

NELSON MAINE

Nelson Maine was a sportsman who loved the rapids section of the Contoocook River in Henniker. Born in 1913, he was crippled as a youth by polio. This didn't stop him from becoming a success in a construction business in Hillsborough—Yeaton & Maine—and an avid hunter and fisherman. He was a champion skeet shooter and active in the Amateur Trapshooting Association. An avid guitarist, he taught himself how to play by ear, and he built his own guitars. He lived near Freight Train Rapid on the Contoocook and bought land on both sides of the river as well as the water power rights. When kayakers had difficulty finding a legal take-out, Nelson offered access across his land. He was very close to his wife, Rachel, and they died on the same day, January 14, 2004. The fishing access on the north bank of the river is a fitting memorial to this extraordinary man.

Starting at Contoocook Falls Road, the trail passes a few driveways before opening onto serene views of the pool at the head of the whitewater section of the river. About a mile down the road, the whitewater starts, and the river has constant rapids all the way to Brown's Way. The right of way alternates between hanging close to the river and making cuts through the gorge wall where the road and river diverge. At the north end, Brown's Way climbs steeply out of the Contoocook gorge, and the river settles into gentler rapids and pools.

Roger Belson kayaking down the rapids at spring high water (Ed Smith, Sportstop Photography)

SW15. Henniker Junction Tour

Ramsdell Road to former bridge site, Henniker, 2.3 miles

Trail condition: ★ ★ ★ Combination of dirt path and paved road, sometimes rough. Poison ivy grows in abundance in this area, so be wary.

Scenery: ★ ★ ★ ★ River views, open fields, and houses in an historic corner of Henniker.

Permitted uses: Non-motorized travel plus snowmobiles; ATVs and motorized trail bikes are not allowed.

Right of way owned by: Army Corps of Engineers (as part of the Hopkinton Flood Control Project).

Maintained by: Army Corps of Engineers.

ACCESS

The western access is at Ramsdell Road off of Route 114, about a half mile south of the 114 bridge over the Contoocook in Henniker center. The Ramsdell Road bridge over the river has been closed; it was under reconstruction in

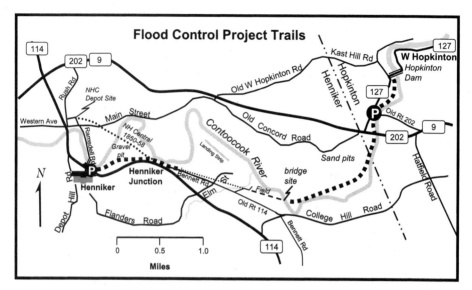

Flood Control Project Trails

the fall of 2007. To be safe, approach Ramsdell Road from the south side of the river. There is parking by the bridge. The eastern access is where the tour (old Route 114) intersects Elm Street.

DESCRIPTION

Jim Sindelar explored the remains of Henniker Junction with me in 2007. We never found the precise location of the junction where the New Hampshire Central Railroad met the Contoocook Valley Railroad. Much of the Contoocook Valley right of way was impassible; but our trip took us through such an interesting part of Henniker that it is worth reporting here.

Starting at the Ramsdell Road bridge, you soon come to a trail fork. Take the left fork to get up to the railroad grade. For a short distance you pass high over the Contoocook River, with fine views. Then you move away from the river and pass over a roller coaster section.

Next comes a large clearing. At first we thought this might be the remains of Henniker Junction. On closer examination, it appears to be the remains of a gravel pit that lowered the terrain. The trail forks again at the pit. The right-hand fork, marked by the remains of some railroad ties, regains the railroad grade.

The trail climbs steadily until it gets close to Route 114. Almost nothing remains of Henniker Junction, marked only by a cement post. Locals say the cement base of the water tower is in this area, but you must know exactly where to look under the leaf mulch.

Surprisingly, the path the New Hampshire Central took to cross the river is easily traced from the junction. Proceed on foot northwest from the monument along a massive fill to the Contoocook River crossing. No signs of the bridge remain.

This cement monument in the woods on the north side of the trail marks Henniker Junction.

Returning to Henniker Junction, the trail along the Contoocook Valley right of way continues and merges with Bennett Road, the old alignment of Route 114. It appears to dead-end on the road, with development obliterating the right of way. Continue along Bennett Road, a quiet street with little traffic, as you proceed to Elm Street.

Take a side trip down Elm to admire the historic buildings. The railroad grade crosses Elm close to Bennett Street, but it is overgrown beyond recognition and is fenced off.

No problem. Go back to Bennett Street and continue east on the old Route 114 grade. You have smooth pavement for a trail! When you come to a dirt road that heads toward the Contoocook, take a left. This road meets the railroad right of way and follows it for a short distance before turning left into a farm field.

The field is one of many in the area that were acquired by the Army Corps of Engineers as part of the Hopkinton Dam project. The Corps leases them to farmers who keep them open.

At first it looks as if you could proceed along the railroad grade from here to the missing river bridge. However, the poison ivy is ferocious, so a better approach is to follow the edge of the farm field parallel to the railroad right of way. Poison ivy stops you from getting all the way to the river. It is possible to see the bridge abutment on the other side of the river, the end point of the next trail (SW16).

Utility lines now use the New Hampshire Central fill leading to the river. Although cleared near the river, the fill is wooded near Henniker Junction.

Army Corps field near the Contoocook River. The dirt road veers to the left here. The railroad right of way is just to the right and is "protected" by poison ivy.

The bridge over the Contoocook was a long one, as the railroad crossed at an angle. There must have been at least one pier in the river. Surprisingly, there is little sign of the bridge today. The Army Corps of Engineers not only removed the bridge, but also took out most of the stone and concrete. All that remains is the abutment on the east side and a few pieces of granite on the west side.

SW16. Hopkinton Dam to Former Bridge Site

See the Flood Control Project Trails map, page 118

Hopkinton Flood Control Dam, Hopkinton, to former bridge site, Henniker, 2.1 miles

Trail condition: ★ ★ ★ Mixture of easy hardpack driveway stretches and more rustic sections with sticks on the trail; some challenge getting by the Route 202 bridge.

Scenery: ★ ★ ★ ★ Woods and nice river views.

Permitted uses: Non-motorized travel plus snowmobiles; ATVs and motorized trail bikes are not allowed.

Right of way owned by: Army Corps of Engineers (as part of the Hopkinton Flood Control Project).
Maintained by: Army Corps of Engineers, driveway users, and a snowmobile club.

ACCESS

Take Route 127 south from Hopkinton Dam or north from Route 202. Turn east on an old paved road just north of Route 202. This is the old Route 202 and leads to its former bridge site, where the concrete abutments still stand. There is room to park near the western abutment.

DESCRIPTION

This short trail is remarkably pretty and feels quite remote. It would be a great place to bring the family for a picnic by the river. The trail follows close by the river and offers excellent water views. It is very clear why this rail line was called the Contoocook Valley Railroad.

The Hopkinton Dam gives this view of the Contoocook River.

Trail along the Contoocook River south of Route 202

It is difficult to get by the new Route 202 bridge.

My description starts at the dam end of the trail. This is a large, earth-fill dam typical of the Army Corps' flood control projects in New England. It can (and does occasionally) back up a considerable height of water, thereby flooding large areas. The Corps had to buy up the land that can be flooded, resulting in a large, park-like region.

The first part of the trail is the driveway used to maintain the dam; it is in excellent shape. The trail then gets rougher, with debris strewn on it. Sticks on the trail may be deposited by high water from dam backup.

The new Route 202 bridge is a handsome structure. Unfortunately, it was not built with the trail in mind and has a steep slope of granite slabs all the way to the river. A snowmobile club constructed a boardwalk to get around it, but high water had ripped it up when I scouted. Until the boardwalk gets repaired, this will be a difficult and dangerous crossing.

Past the Route 202 bridge, the trail continues through the woods and along the river. A driveway heads off to a local gravel pit, and you pass a pump and pipe that send water to that operation. The trail dead-ends at the missing bridge across the river. From the bridge abutment—an excellent lunch spot— you get a fine view of the river.

Southeast Region

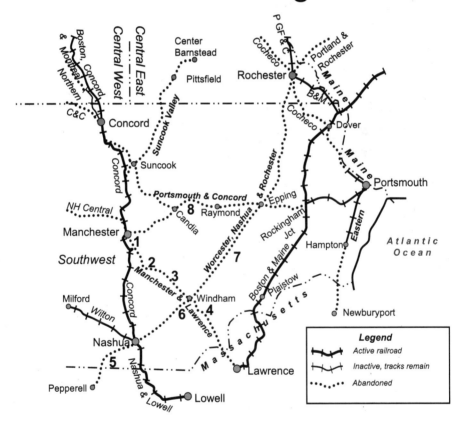

THE Southeast Region extends from the Merrimack River east to the Maine border and Atlantic Ocean, and from the Massachusetts border north to Concord, Barnstead, and Rochester.

This region has always had a close relationship with nearby Boston. Three of its early railroads were extensions of Massachusetts lines: the Nashua & Lowell

The Southeast Region is low and flat, with numerous wetlands views like this one from the Freemont Branch Trail.

(1838), Eastern (1840), and Boston & Maine (1843). Another, the Concord Railroad, was built in 1838 as a purely New Hampshire railroad.

The Eastern and the Boston & Maine waged an epic struggle for control over the lucrative traffic between Boston and Portland. The tracks of the winner, the B&M, are still in use from Lawrence, MA, to Dover, while only a short stub of the loser's are in use.

The other Southeast Region railroads had smaller markets for passenger and freight traffic. All were swallowed up by the B&M in the railroad consolidations of the late nineteenth century.

This region is relatively flat and low, so you will see many scenic wetlands views from these rail trails. There is much work to be done to realize their full potential. However, you can enjoy many appealing stretches while this work proceeds.

Manchester & Lawrence Railroad

Lawrence, MA, to Manchester
Built: 1848–49
Abandoned: Salem–Londonderry, 1983, 1986; Londonderry–Manchester, 2000

On paper, this railroad looked like a winner. It connected the major cities of Manchester and Lawrence. It offered a more direct route for traffic from Boston to Manchester, Concord, and beyond. Yet it never enjoyed the success of the Concord and the Nashua & Lowell lines. Perhaps that is to be expected, since the Concord operated it!

Built in 1848 and 1849, the line was operated mostly by the Concord Railroad before being leased to the Boston & Maine Railroad in 1887. A short spur built to Rockingham Park brought Boston area fans to the trotting races. Passenger service continued to Manchester until 1953 and to Rockingham Park until 1960. Freight service continued to the mid 1980s, when the Salem to

Derry segment was abandoned. Today the entire corridor has been abandoned by the railroad, and most of the rails are gone.

The state of New Hampshire purchased 23 miles of right of way for a rail trail. It has great importance in providing local greenways for the populous towns it passes through. It also offers the possibility of a lengthy alternative transportation route, allowing commuters to ride bicycles to work or school.

Trail quality varies considerably on the Manchester-to-Salem corridor.

Four trail maps in this section cover the 20 miles from Manchester to the Massachusetts border, with an additional detail map for Derry. The railroad grade is now a patchwork of trail segments. Fine paved stretches in Manchester, Derry, and Windham are separated by forlorn and forgotten stretches in between. Efforts are now underway to connect them to achieve the extended trail promise.

In order to point out the different status of each trail segment, I have divided the Manchester-to-Salem corridor into the following sections, roughly by town:

- ◆ SE1. South Manchester Trailway (Beech Street–Gold Street), Manchester

- ◆ Proposed continuation of South Manchester Trailway (Gold Street–Perimeter Road, Manchester)

- ◆ Perimeter Road, Manchester, to Sanborn Road, Londonderry (possible trail)

- SE2. Londonderry Rail Trail (Sanborn Road–Route 28)

- Route 28, Londonderry, to Hood Park, Derry (blocked trail in need of work)

- SE3. Derry Rail Trail (Hood Park–Windham town line)

- SE4. Windham Rail Trail

- Proposed Salem Trail

The importance of this corridor was pointed out in a 2003 state report, the *Salem to Concord Bikeway Feasibility Study* (available from the New Hampshire Department of Transportation, www.nh.gov/dot). As part of the I-93 widening project, the New Hampshire Department of Transportation proposed constructing a bike path parallel to the highway. The Salem-to-Concord study pointed out that it would make much more sense to make a complete trail out of the Manchester & Lawrence Railroad right of way. However, difficult problems must be solved to connect the Londonderry segment with the Manchester and Derry trails.

For the Londonderry-to-Manchester connection, the feasibility study recommended using Grenier Field Road and Mammoth Road to go from Sanborn Road in Londonderry to Harvey Road and Perimeter Road in Manchester (see

A trolley like this one went through the Little Cohas Brook wetlands. (Courtesy of Karen Booth Photography)

View of the railroad crossing of Little Cohas Brook from the trolley right of way

the South Manchester Trailway and Londonderry Rail Trail maps). I would prefer the option of going through the scenic wetlands of Little Cohas Brook. Unfortunately, the railroad right of way from Route 28 to a quarter mile west of Mammoth Road is privately owned, with buildings and driveways on it. Another possibility is using an existing path on the right of way of the Manchester Street Railway, a trolley line built in 1871, which connected Manchester with Derry. Perhaps the right answer is a combination of the trolley and railroad lines. However, none of these will happen without an activist group working with landowners, the town, and the Trails Bureau.

The primary problem in linking the Londonderry and Derry trails is a blockage at Madden Road (see the Londonderry Rail Trail map). Madden Road, which is the driveway to a small industrial site, is built on a fill crossing the railroad right of way. Its name is easy to remember, as the fill blocking the trail is maddening! On the south side of Madden Road, the railroad right of way crosses High Street and proceeds on the front lawn of a condominium complex. Because of these problems, the trail is not maintained between Route 28 in Londonderry and Hood Park in Derry; it is rocky and still has some track. A new group, the Derry Rail Trail Alliance, may work with the Trails Bureau to improve this stretch.

　　　　　New Hampshire Rail Trails

HANDS ACROSS THE MERRIMACK TRAIL CONNECTIONS

Manchester has ambitious plans to link many of the city's trails. The map below shows some of the near-term links.

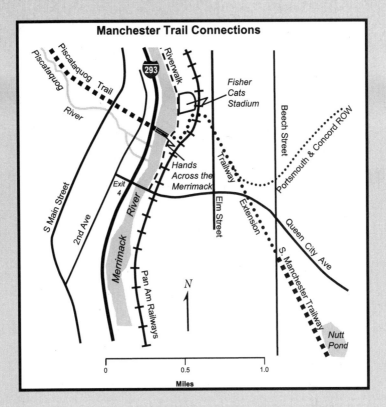

The Queen City Trail Alliance plans to extend the South Manchester Trailway north from Beech Street through the tunnel under Elm Street to connect with the Hands Across the Merrimack's pedestrian bridge (under construction in 2007–08). This bridge will be a remodeling of the New Hampshire Central Railroad bridge, and hence will connect directly to the Piscataquog (SW13) and Goffstown (SW12) Trails. The Riverwalk, a paved pedestrian path on the east side of the Merrimack River, will have a connecting path to the bridge. Longer-term, the hope is to connect with the Portsmouth Branch Trail (SE8) using the Portsmouth & Concord Railroad corridor.

The Riverwalk passes under the Hands Across the Merrimack bridge.

The railroad bridge was solid but needed decking and railings.

There is also some good news for this corridor: in 2008 the Hands Across the Merrimack project will connect the Goffstown Rail Trail (SW12) and Piscataquog Trail (SW13) with an extension of the South Manchester Trailway, the northern end of the Manchester & Lawrence corridor. This will eventually support rail trails from the New Hampshire border in Salem all the way to the center of Goffstown.

SE1. South Manchester Trailway

Beech Street to Gold Street, Manchester, 1 mile.
Trail condition: ★ ★ ★ ★ ★ New pavement.
Scenery: ★ ★ ★ ★ Nicely landscaped urban greenway with access to Nutt Pond and Precourt Park.
Permitted uses: Non-motorized travel.
Right of way owned by: State of New Hampshire; trail easement granted to the Manchester Parks & Recreation Department.
Maintained by: City of Manchester and the Queen City Trail Alliance.

ACCESS
Take the Brown Avenue exit off Interstate 293/Route 101 and proceed a short distance north to Beech Street. Take a right at the Manchester Commons shopping center, which includes Shaw's market and a New Hampshire Division of Motor Vehicles office, and park in the lot. The trail starts there. Alternatively, you can park at Precourt Park, which is accessible from Route 28.

DESCRIPTION
This urban greenway is the result of a remarkable effort led by John St. Hilaire to protect the railroad corridor when Manchester was about to let Shaw's Supermarkets take it over for a new market. This activism not only led to the trail we have today, but Shaw's saw the value of the trail and contributed to its construction.

North of Shaw's, the right of way was an impenetrable jungle. However, the Queen City Trail Alliance cleared it in 2007 as a first step toward reaching the Hands Across the Merrimack Bridge.

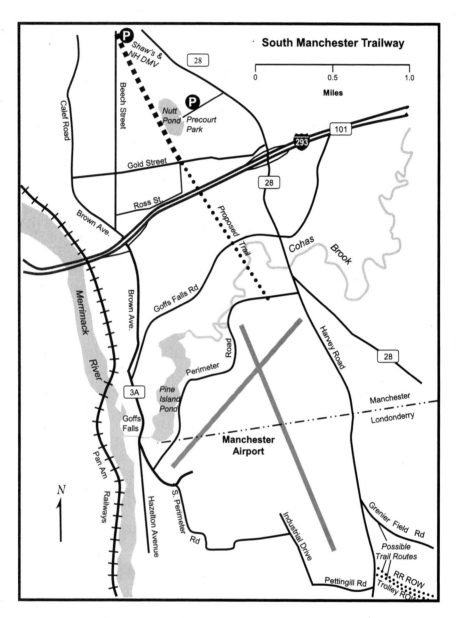

In contrast, the new section is already a paved and landscaped trail. Since this section is only a mile, I recommend you take your time, stroll into Precourt Park, and view Nutt Pond.

The trail starts here to the right of Shaw's Supermarket. Trash was cleaned up and the path attractively landscaped.

Side trails lead to Precourt Park and Nutt Pond.

Proposed Continuation of South Manchester Trailway
Gold Street–Perimeter Road, Manchester

The Queen City Trail Alliance is working to extend the South Manchester Trailway to Perimeter Road. Although in poor shape now, this section is critically important for making a through trail from Manchester to Salem. It needs landscaping, decking and railings on the Cohas Brook bridge, and improvement of the trail surface. The Queen City Trail Alliance has completed the engineering design. At this point, though, this part of the Manchester & Lawrence corridor is nearly as unattractive as a town dump.

When renovated as a pedestrian bridge, the Cohas Brook Trestle will be a major attraction on the South Manchester Trailway.

The trestle bridge over Cohas Brook is impressive and would present a view of the Cohas Brook valley if it were accessible. Both ends are now closed off with chain link fencing, and the north end has suffered minor fire damage.

SE2. Londonderry Rail Trail

Sanborn Road to Route 28, Londonderry, 3.2 miles

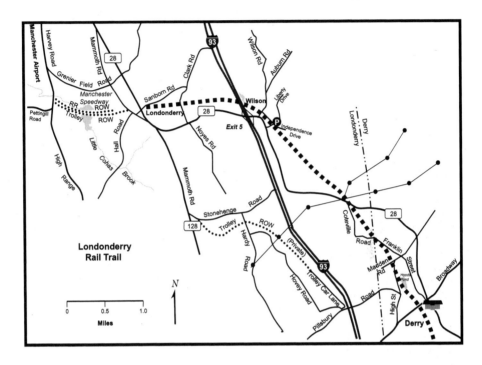

Trail condition: ★ ★ ★ Roller coasters, washouts, and sometimes water on the trail, but certainly passable on foot or mountain bike.

Scenery: ★ ★ ★ Some nice wetlands views, but currently trashy and needs landscaping.

Permitted uses: Non-motorized travel year-round; snowmobiles, ATVs, and motorized trail bikes in winter when snow-covered.

Right of way owned by: State of New Hampshire.

Maintained by: Trails Bureau, but they need assistance from activists who will champion the trail.

ACCESS

The only real parking area along this segment of trail is along Independence Drive at its intersection with Auburn Road, about two-tenths of a mile east of I-93 Exit 5. On my weekday scout, it was filled with cars, perhaps serving as

Problems like this eroded spot are typical of the Londonderry Rail Trail.

a "Park & Ride" site. It should be more available on weekends. The northern trailhead is at Sanborn Road, very close to Route 28. It has no parking. On the southern end, Route 28 provides access, but there is no parking.

DESCRIPTION

The Trails Bureau does its best with limited resources, but it relies heavily on volunteer groups to maintain the rail trails. When no group volunteers, the result is trash, washouts, poor drainage, and lack of signage, giving the impression that the corridor is worthless. In fact, the opposite is the case with the Londonderry Rail Trail. This trail should be a popular greenway and is important for continuity of the overall Manchester-to-Salem trail system.

Starting at Sanborn Road, here is what I found in my scouting. I hope improvements will be apparent by the time you explore this trail. I felt like a pioneer, putting up with roller coasters, severely eroded sections, and "ponds" in the middle of the trail that required a detour. Yet there are pretty sections that show the corridor's promise.

I-93 crosses over the railroad grade on high bridges, so there is no problem getting past it. The trail is rough here, however, with more roller coasters.

Auburn Road and the Independence Drive parking area are near the site of the former Wilson railroad station. From here to Route 28, the surface is either cinders or dirt and gravel, but rough. Simply taking a grader through and smoothing out the roller coasters would make this a much more satisfactory trail experience. Some wetlands in this stretch would provide interesting views if you were able to stop looking out for the rough trail in front of you.

As explained in the railroad description, this trail continues past Route 28 but is in poor shape because of the blockage at Madden Road. For now it is best to avoid this stretch and start again at Hood Park in Derry if you wish to continue to the attractive Derry and Windham Rail Trails.

This small pond a few tenths of a mile east of Sanborn Road suggests the scenic possibilities.

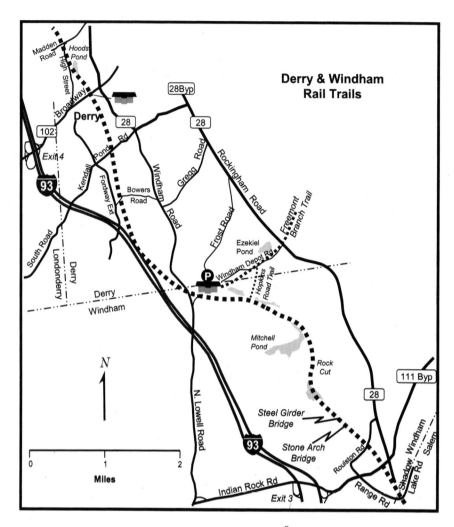

Derry & Windham Rail Trails

SE3. Derry Rail Trail

Hood Park, Derry, to North Lowell Road, Windham, 3.6 miles

Trail condition: In Derry Center: ★★★★★ Paved for 1 mile; outside Derry Center: ★★★★ Dirt surface, mostly in good shape, with a few roller coasters and stony stretches.

Scenery: ★★★★ Interesting combination of Derry Center and more remote settings.

Permitted uses: Non-motorized travel; designed primarily for bicycling and walking. Derry has frequent signs prohibiting OHRVs.

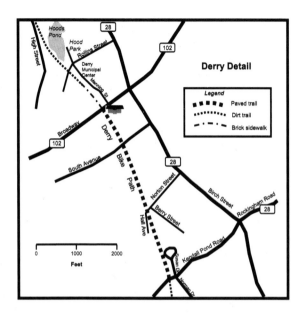

Right of way owned by: Town of Derry.
Maintained by: Town of Derry and the Derry Rail Trail Alliance.

ACCESS

At the northern end, look for a parking spot around Hood Park (see Derry Detail map) or in Derry Center. At the southern end, there is parking at Windham Depot, just over the Windham town line. For detailed driving instructions, see the Windham Rail Trail (SE4) access information.

DESCRIPTION

Derry has done an excellent job making a fine rail trail through town. A mile in the center of town is the Derry Bike Path, paved south of Broadway and an attractive brick sidewalk north of Broadway. Other sections are well maintained dirt trail.

From Hood Park, follow the dirt path until you emerge in Derry Center, near the Derry Municipal Center. At this point, the Derry Bike Path begins. It crosses Broadway and goes by the remodeled Derry Depot, now the Depot Square Steakhouse.

The paved Derry Bike Path, constructed in 2002, starts at the depot. It continues about eight-tenths of a mile and is part of a network of trails connecting all of the schools in Derry. Notice that paved trails like this one attract graffiti

The brick sidewalk becomes a paved trail by the Depot Square Steakhouse, Derry's renovated railroad depot.

artists. The paved trail is pleasant but unspectacular as it goes through suburban neighborhoods to Kendall Pond Road. There, the trail becomes a dirt path again.

At Bowers Road the trail goes through a small culvert that is just large enough for a person to walk through with a bicycle. The Derry Rail Trail Alliance is working to pave the section of trail between the Derry Bike Path and the Windham Rail Trail. This project may include improving the passage across Bowers Road.

The next one and a half miles proceed through a rural setting with some wetlands. Even when the trail gets close to I-93, a strip of woods separates it from the highway. At the Derry-Windham town line, you come to North Lowell Road, where the paved Windham Rail Trail (SE4) begins.

SE4. Windham Rail Trail

See Derry and Windham Rail Trails map, page 140.

North Lowell Road to Range Road (old Route 111), Windham, 4.1 miles

Trail condition: ★★★★★ New paved trail with hardpack equestrian path alongside.

Scenery: ★★★★★ Cuts and fills with wetlands views.

Permitted uses: Non-motorized travel year-round; snowmobiles, ATVs, and motorized trail bikes in winter when snow-covered. A five-foot stone-dust shoulder encourages equestrian use.

Right of way owned by: State of New Hampshire.

Maintained by: Windham Rail Trail Alliance.

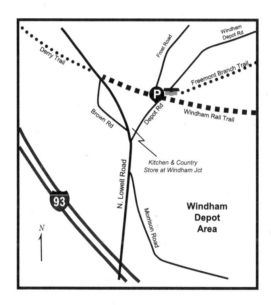

ACCESS

The best northern access is at Windham Depot. Coming from the south, take Exit 3 off of I-93, go west on Indian Rock Road, and turn right (north) onto North Lowell Road (Windham Road in Derry). Turn right onto Depot Road at the Kitchen & Country Store at Windham Junction. When facing the restored Boston & Maine caboose, parking is on the right at the depot and freight house.

Parking is allowed at Windham Depot only during daylight hours (half hour before sunrise to half hour after sunset).

To reach Windham Depot from the north, take Exit 4 off of I-93. Proceed east on Broadway and turn south on Birch Street, in the center of town. This is Route 28, although not labeled as such at this intersection. At the stoplight where 28 takes a left, go straight onto Windham Road. Follow Windham Road across the Windham line, where it becomes North Lowell Road. Take your first left in Windham onto Depot Road. If you see the I-93 overpass, you have overshot Depot Road.

Windham's depot and freight house are currently in disrepair, but restoration is coming. The depot is unusual in that it faced both railroads, which crossed at a forty-five-degree angle.

The southern access is off of I-93 Exit 3, as shown on the Derry and Windham Rail Trails map. After completion of the Route 111 bypass, scheduled for 2008, the trail will cross a new bridge over the bypass and end at Range Road. Until then, the trail ends at Roulston Road. Roulston has been chopped up by the new highway construction, making this access to the trail very confusing and changeable at the time of this writing. Either ask a local for directions or backtrack to Windham Depot.

DESCRIPTION

I'll admit to a bias against paved trails, but this one is gorgeous and well worth experiencing. As you proceed along it, you can thank Mark Samsel and the Windham Trail Alliance for two major accomplishments. The first was reclaiming the trail from off-highway recreational vehicle use. ATVs and trail

Rock and earth cuts and the view toward Mitchell Pond are some of the highlights of the Windham Rail Trail.

The Windham Trail includes a hardpack equestrian path beside the paved trail.

bikes dug up the dirt surface and created an unpleasant environment for walkers, bicyclists, and equestrian users. OHRVs are now banned except when the trail has snow cover. The second major accomplishment was turning a poor stretch of trail into a well-maintained, landscaped, and trash-free trail worth using. This required dedicated planning, hard work, and generous participation of local sponsors.

For an encore, the group is working to restore the station and freight house at Windham Depot. Using a Transportation Enhancement grant, they plan to complete the renovation of the two buildings and improve the parking lot in 2009 or 2010.

The trail proceeds through cuts and fills, with wetlands views from the fill stretches. One of the earth cuts has an impressive masonry retaining wall. There is a handsome stone arch bridge over an abandoned road about a third of a mile before Roulston Road. It is well hidden from the trail user. To find it, take a short path at the southwest corner of a steel girder bridge over another abandoned road. At the bottom of the railroad fill, turn right for the steel bridge and left for the stone arch bridge.

At the southern end, you can complete your journey at Roulston Road or continue over the new Route 111 bypass (after completion in 2008) to Range Road at the Salem border. This is the old Route 111 and not a good trailhead.

Proposed Salem Trail

Range Road (old Route 111) to the Massachusetts border, 5.1 miles

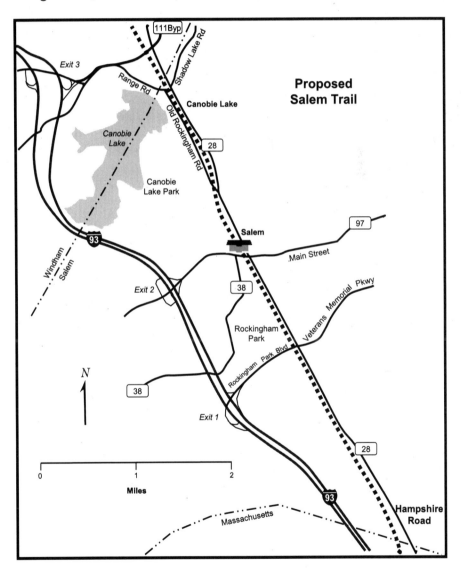

A renovated depot and scenic wetlands may anchor a new Salem rail trail greenway, which would also provide shopping and commuter access to south Salem businesses.

The Manchester & Lawrence corridor in Salem is owned by the state but is currently closed to the public due to dangerous road crossings.

The town of Salem is working to make the railroad bed into a paved trail. This will create an alternative transportation corridor that provides convenient access to stores and light industry off of busy Route 28. Trees across the trail, light industry use of the right of way, and monotonous scenery south of Rockingham Park are current challenges to trail development.

Using a Congestion Mitigation and Air Quality Grant, the town undertook an engineering study of the entire Salem stretch of the railroad corridor. Moreover, a volunteer group is working to renovate the Salem Depot.

Worcester, Nashua & Rochester Railroad

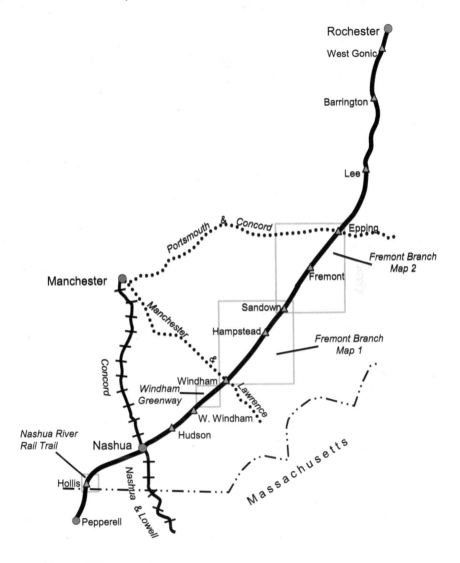

Worcester, MA, to Rochester
Built: Worcester–Nashua, 1846–48; Nashua–Rochester, 1871–74
Abandoned: Epping–West Gonic, 1935; Hudson–Fremont, 1935; Hollis–Hudson, 1942; Fremont–Epping, 1982

This railroad line was a good idea at the wrong time. Unsuccessful financially as a railroad, parts of the corridor now have a new incarnation as scenic rail trails.

The Worcester & Nashua Railroad was one of the early lines, constructed 1846–48. The extension between Nashua and Rochester came much later, in 1871–74. The extended railroad was then renamed the Worcester, Nashua & Rochester (WN&R). It hoped to compete with the Eastern and Boston & Maine for traffic between Massachusetts and Maine. However, the freight traffic went to the shorter lines by the coast, especially given the price wars between the B&M and Eastern. Furthermore, the extension of the line to Rochester caused the railroad to take on a debt burden that weakened it financially.

The B&M took over the WN&R by lease in 1887, calling it the Worcester, Nashua & Portland Division. Under B&M control, the line had its heyday around the turn of the century. Eighteen freight and six passenger trains passed the Sandown depot daily. Freight included lumber and wood products, milk, shoes, coal, and household supplies. The *Bar Harbor* and *State of Maine* passenger trains took vacationers to their destinations along the Maine Coast. By the 1930s, however, the line had very little traffic. The B&M abandoned most of it in 1935.

Much of the railroad right of way was taken over by highways. Route 111 occupies most of the distance from Hudson to Windham. Route 125 occupies the stretch from Epping to Barrington. Fortunately, a long segment from Windham Depot to Epping has been saved by the state as the Fremont Branch Trail. A two-mile stretch in Windham exists as a town-owned greenway, and the first mile from the Massachusetts border recently became an extension of the Nashua River Rail Trail out of Ayer, MA.

SE5. Nashua River Rail Trail: New Hampshire Extension

Massachusetts border to Gilson Road, Nashua, 1 mile
Trail condition: ★ ★ ★ ★ ★ Paved, with grass shoulders.
Scenery: ★ ★ ★ Nicely landscaped trail in a suburban setting.
Permitted uses: Non-motorized travel.
Right of way owned by: City of Nashua.
Maintained by: Nashua Division of Public Works.

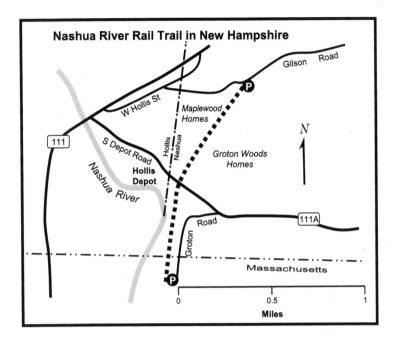

Nashua River Rail Trail in New Hampshire

Gilson Road

W Hollis St

Maplewood Homes

111

S Depot Road

Hollis Nashua

Groton Woods Homes

N

Hollis Depot

Nashua River

111A

Groton Road

Massachusetts

0   0.5   1

Miles

ACCESS

There are excellent parking facilities off Groton Road at the state boundary and off Gilson Road on the north end.

DESCRIPTION

The Nashua River Rail Trail is a first class rail trail in Massachusetts, which was completed in 2002. This ten-foot-wide paved trail goes eleven miles from Ayer through Groton, Pepperell, and Dunstable, MA.

In 2006 the trail was extended a mile into New Hampshire in a project funded largely by a local real estate developer (Homes by Paradise). This is a prime example of a rail trail significantly increasing the value of abutting real estate.

You can find descriptions of the Massachusetts trail on the internet. This brief entry describes just the New Hampshire extension.

At the northern end, there is an attractive park with a lake and a side path leading from the rail trail. In the middle, the trail passes by two developments of single-family homes built by Homes by Paradise. Maplewood is northwest of the trail and Groton Woods is to the southeast. Design of both took advan-

View of the paved trail and grass shoulders near Gilson Road

tage of the trail as an integral part of the landscaping. You will therefore be walking or riding in the middle of a well-landscaped portion of suburbia.

Moreover, it provides two excellent trailheads with parking for a more extensive ride through the Massachusetts portion of the trail or a greenway for a picnic lunch or stroll with your dog.

SE6. Windham Greenway

Beacon Hill Road to Nashua Road, Windham, 2 miles
Trail condition: ★★★ Rocks, ruts, and standing water make this a challenge.
Scenery: ★★★★ Ponds and woods.
Permitted uses: Non-motorized travel and snowmobiles; ATVs and motorized trail bikes explicitly prohibited.
Right of way owned by: Town of Windham
Maintained by: Not yet maintained. Windham's efforts to date have concentrated on the Windham Rail Trail (SE4).

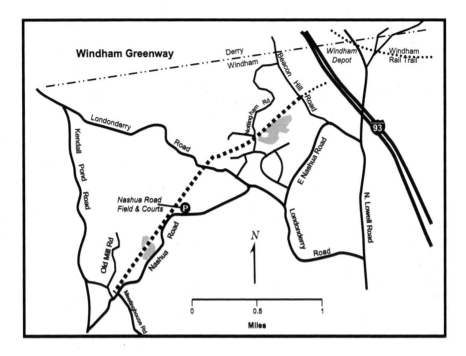

ACCESS

The northern access is easy to find. Take North Lowell Road (Windham Road in Derry) south from Route 28 in Derry or north from Route 111 in Windham. Near the I-93 overpass, turn west onto East Nashua Road and continue on Beacon Hill Road. The trail crossing is at a dip in the road about one-fifth mile from East Nashua Road. There is also good access at both Londonderry Road and the Nashua Road Field and Courts, where parking is available. The southern end, unfortunately, is hard to find. The trail does not go all the way to a road, but a small path leads down to it from Nashua Road near Meetinghouse Road.

DESCRIPTION

This section of the Worcester, Nashua & Rochester Railroad right of way, owned by the town of Windham, is ideally suited to be a local greenway. It passes by two ponds, town sports facilities, and a densely populated area of Windham. All it needs is improvement of the trail surface, which is currently a mess. Only two miles long, it is unlikely to attract many users from outside of Windham.

One of two scenic ponds the trail passes.

From Beacon Hill Road, the railroad grade goes north about a quarter-mile to I-93, but the rough path and pools of water discourage use of this dead-end stretch.

Going south, the trail immediately traverses the western bank of a large pond. A severely eroded culvert here has caused a few feet of the railroad bed to wash out, leaving a shallow ditch that requires bicyclists to dismount.

Past Nottingham Road, the trail is extremely rocky from erosion as it passes by a brook and goes through the woods. Pools of water blocked the trail just north of Londonderry Road when I scouted in May 2007. South of Londonderry Road, the trail has ruts with standing water and is quite rocky.

You pass the Nashua Road Field (for soccer and lacrosse) and the Nashua Road Courts (for tennis and basketball) where Nashua Road comes close to the trail. Providing good off-road access to these facilities should be enough reason for Windham to improve the trail surface. Moreover, the facility parking provides good access to the greenway.

South of the town sports facilities, you come to the second pond. The trail traverses one side of the pond on a fill, and Nashua Road passes on the other side.

From there the trail surface is well drained and in good condition until it ends abruptly near the intersection of Nashua and Meetinghouse Roads. Take a small path to the left to get up to Nashua Road.

The scenery is good, but the trail surface needs work.

SE7. Fremont Branch Trail (Rockingham Recreational Trail)

Windham Depot, Windham, to Main Street, Epping, 18.5 miles
Trail condition: ★★★ Tough going because of sandy surface.
Scenery: ★★★★★ Wetlands, spruce swamps, woods, and fields; restored depot at Sandown; a few spots have trash dumps.
Permitted uses: Non-motorized travel year-round and snowmobiles in winter. ATVs and motorized trail bikes are allowed year-round from Route 28 to Route 107 and in the winter when snow covered from Route 107 to Epping.

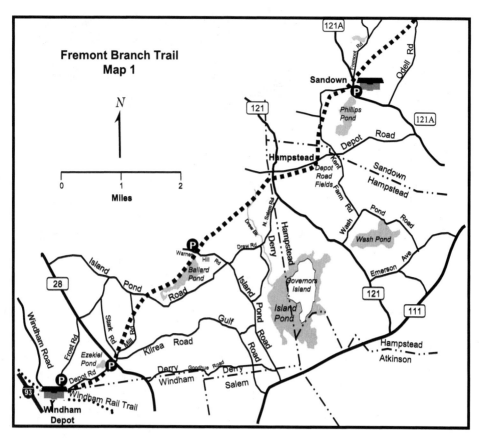

Right of way owned by: State of New Hampshire.
Maintained by: Trails Bureau.

ACCESS

The best access points are Windham Depot (see access notes for Windham Rail Trail, SE4); Route 28 and Warner Hill Road in Derry; the depot in Sandown; Route 107 in Fremont; and the trailhead in Epping. The only official Trails Bureau parking area is on Warner Hill Road, but all of the other access points except Epping have usable parking areas. The northern trailhead in Epping is unmarked; use the Epping Trailhead map for orientation and look for roadside parking on Main Street or Railroad Avenue.

The Epping trailhead by AmeriGas Propane is unmarked.

DESCRIPTION

The Fremont Branch Trail is one of the state's most scenic paths, as it traverses a region with many unspoiled ponds, wetlands, and spruce swamps. However, it is not an easy trail to walk or ride, due to miles of heavy sand on the trail.

Most of the trail is open to off-highway recreational vehicles. Since they were prohibited from the Windham Rail Trail, this trail became particularly popular for ATVs and trail bike riders. They are not allowed near Windham Depot or north of Route 107 in Fremont in the non-winter months.

If you plan to bike the entire trail or hike a long length, it is definitely a good idea to plant a car at both ends of your route. You won't want to ride round trip over all that sand! Alternatively, ride the trail from Windham Depot to Sandown and from Sandown to Epping on separate outings, as Sandown is about the midpoint of this 18.5-mile trail.

WHAT IS THE ROCKINGHAM RECREATIONAL TRAIL?

Both the Portsmouth Branch and the Freemont Branch Trails have signs labeling them the "Rockingham Recreational Trail." The Trails Bureau web site distinguishes the individual trails with a modifier, such as "Rockingham Recreational Trail, Fremont Branch." In order to be clear about which trail in the system I am talking about, I use the modifier names given by the Trails Bureau.

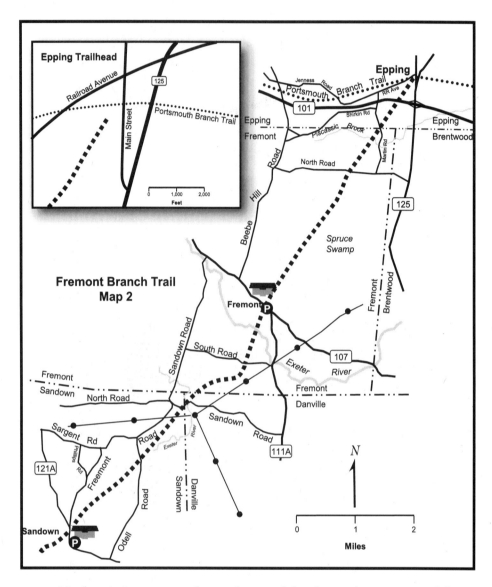

Epping Trailhead

Railroad Avenue

125

Main Street

Portsmouth Branch Trail

0   1,000   2,000
Feet

**Fremont Branch Trail
Map 2**

Jenness Road

Portsmouth Branch Trail

Epping

101

RR Ave

Shirkin Rd

Epping
Fremont

Piscassic Brook

Martin Rd

North Road

Epping
Brentwood

125

Spruce
Swamp

Beebe Hill

Fremont

P

Fremont
Brentwood

Sandown Road

South Road

Exeter
River

107

Fremont
Danville

Fremont
Sandown

North Road

Sandown
Road

Fremont

Sargent Rd

Road

Jenkey

Sandown

111A

Phillips Rd

Exeter

N

121A

Freemont

Road

Exeter
Danville
Sandown

Danville
Sandown

0   1   2

Sandown

P

Odell

Miles

My description starts at the southern end, by the northeast corner of the Windham Depot. In 2007 a sand pile and highway department equipment obscured the trailhead, so you may have to look for it.

The trail moves quickly into the woods, which give it a remote feeling. Past the Windham Depot Road crossing, the trail skirts Ezekiel Pond.

Bertha Deveau, right, curator of the Sandown Historical Society,
and Barbara Crawford, left, gave the author an excellent tour of the
renovated depot and train cars when he scouted this trail.

There is a small parking area at the Route 28 crossing. Then it is back to the
woods. After crossing Mill Road and Island Pond Road, you come to a long,
shallow, unspoiled lake called Ballard Pond.

Ballard Pond is typical of the pond and wetlands views on the Fremont Branch Trail.

The next few miles north of Warner Hill Road are especially scenic and worth the effort required to keep struggling on the sand. A mile past Hampstead's Depot Road Fields, you can just barely make out Phillips Pond in the distance, viewed through wetlands.

The Fremont depot on Route 107 is now a private residence.
Parking is available across the highway.

       New Hampshire Rail Trails

In Sandown, the local historical society has renovated the depot. The exhibits and rolling stock are worth a stop to look around. As the trail goes through a tiny corner of Danville, you come to a small stream that is the upper Exeter River. Beyond South Road, you cross the river again.

At Route 107 in Fremont there is a large parking lot. It is needed for ATVs, since this is the northern trailhead for their use, but is open to all trail users. North of Route 107, there are several miles of unusual spruce swamp wetlands up to North Road. The scenery then changes to large farms with open fields.

The trail diverges off the railroad grade to go under Route 101 and then continues to the Epping trailhead just southwest of the intersection of Main Street with the Portsmouth Branch Trail.

Portsmouth & Concord Railroad

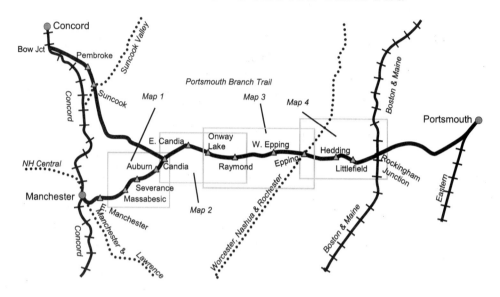

Concord and Manchester to Portsmouth

Built: 1847–62

Abandoned: Candia–Suncook, 1862; Bow Jct.–Suncook, 1953; East Manchester–Rockingham Jct., 1982

The Portsmouth & Concord Railroad was constructed slowly between those two cities from 1847 to 1852. The financial problems that delayed construction continued, and the line was taken over by the Concord Railroad in 1858. To prevent competition for the Concord's Manchester-to-Concord line, Concord management built a new connection from Candia to Manchester and ripped out the track between Candia and Suncook. The remaining Bow Junction-to-Suncook section became part of the Suncook Valley line.

The line served the cotton and wool mills in Manchester, providing both freight and passenger service. It became part of the Concord & Montreal Railroad when that line was formed by the merger of the Concord and the Boston, Concord & Montreal in 1889. Then the Boston & Maine Railroad gained control of the C&M in 1895.

The B&M abandoned most of the line (East Manchester to Rockingham Junction) in 1982. The state of New Hampshire bought the right of way, so it is now available as an important rail trail. The remaining Rockingham Junction-to-Portsmouth stretch is still in use, providing the only railroad access to Portsmouth.

The state gave the city of Manchester title to the right of way west of Page Street in Manchester. The city is now investigating how to turn this corridor into a trail that would connect Massabesic Lake with the trails on the Manchester & Lawrence Railroad corridor. Located in a high density section of Manchester, this greenway would become an important recreation and alternative transportation facility for the city. With Mayor Frank Guinta promoting this project, it has a good chance of succeeding.

From Page Street to Massabesic Lake, there are 1.8 miles of poorly maintained trail. A large culvert provides passage under I-93, but Peabody Avenue, about halfway into this stretch, is an obstacle that explains the lack of trail maintenance. The road is built on a steep fill that blocks the railroad corridor. When Manchester makes a greenway out of the stretch between the South Manchester Trailway and Page Street, it will become important to upgrade this trail continuation to Massabesic.

MANCHESTER–CONCORD TRAIL CONNECTION

As part of the Interstate 93 widening project, the New Hampshire Department of Transportation proposed to build a bike path along the highway from Salem north to Concord. Trail activists quickly convinced DOT to use the Manchester & Lawrence Railroad corridor for a trail close to but somewhat away from the highway. The problem was how to get from Manchester to Concord. The 2003 **Salem to Concord Bikeway Feasibility Study** suggests a route that would include the portion of the original Portsmouth & Concord corridor between Suncook and Bow. The study is available from the Bicycle/Pedestrian Coordinator at the New Hampshire Department of Transportation.

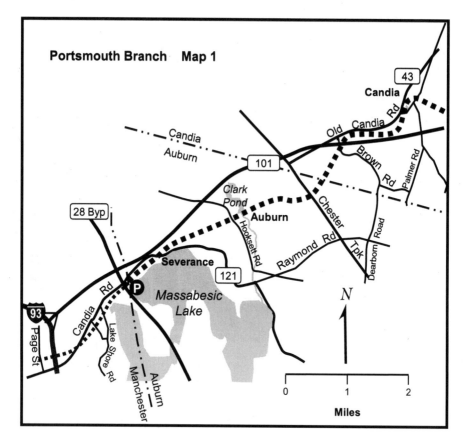

SE8. Portsmouth Branch Trail (Rockingham Recreational Trail)

Route 28 Bypass (Massabesic Lake), Manchester, to Rockingham Jct., Newfields, 25 miles.

Trail condition: ★★★ Often easy going, but rough, muddy, and sandy sections keep this from rating four stars.

Scenery: Massabesic–Raymond: ★★★★★ Lakes, ponds, and wetlands vistas; **Raymond–Rockingham Jct:** ★★★★ Still pleasant, but more built-up.

Permitted uses: Non-motorized travel and snowmobiles; ATVs and motorized trail bikes are prohibited throughout the year. Watch out! This is unusual, as OHRVs are usually allowed on state trails when snowmobiles are.

Right of way owned by: State of New Hampshire.

Massabesic Lake from the trail

Maintained by: Trails Bureau and Southern New Hampshire Snow Slickers.

ACCESS

For the western access at Massabesic Lake, take Route 101 to Exit 1. Head south on Route 28 Bypass (Londonderry Turnpike). Continue south just past the Candia Road circle. The large parking lot for Massabesic Lake is on your left. There is also a large parking area on Depot Street in East Candia. In Raymond parking is available in the center of town on Main Street by the Raymond Historical Society's restored depot.

To find the eastern trailhead, take a close look at the Rockingham Junction Area detail map. From the new Route 108, go north of the two sets of active tracks and turn south on the Old Route 108. Go to the end and park at the old depot. Be sure to avoid parking on the active Pan Am Railways tracks.

DESCRIPTION

This long trail splits almost evenly at Raymond, with twelve miles from Massabesic to Raymond and thirteen from Raymond to Rockingham Junction. The western half is well worth exploring for its outstanding scenery. The eastern

Interstate 93

Route 121

Route 101

Onway Lake Road

Main Street Candia

The Portsmouth Branch Trail goes through numerous culverts to cross under roads and highways. Some have low overhead; all are ugly corrugated metal. They make the trail user nostalgic for the original road overpass bridges.

half is pleasant, especially on the Raymond and Newfields ends. However, it is more built up in Epping and not as scenic there. If you don't have time to take the entire Portsmouth Branch Trail, make sure you explore the Massabesic-to-Raymond section.

The trail is rough in places, but highly negotiable. It is much easier riding than the sandy Fremont Branch Trail (SE7), the other half of the Rockingham Recreational Trail network.

Clark Pond is one of many ponds on the trail.

Massabesic-to-Raymond Section

This section is a gem of a trail, with lakes, ponds, wetlands, and woods. I highly recommend it. Most of the road crossings are through culverts, including some with low overhead and hills leading up to them. A locomotive could never fit through, but they give walkers and bicyclists safe below-grade passage across the roads.

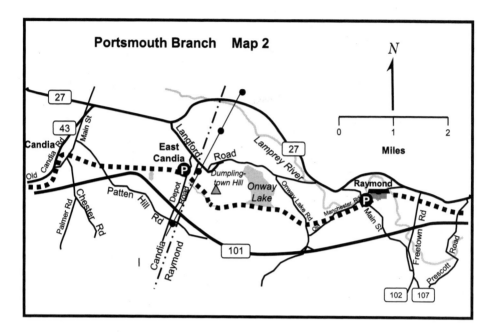

Heading east from the Massabesic Lake parking lot, the trail follows the lake shoreline. The lake's Indian name means "the place of much water." A large lake, Massabesic is the water supply for the city of Manchester.

After crossing under Route 121, the trail departs from the lake. Over the next three and a half miles through Auburn to Route 101, it skirts several small ponds and associated wetlands, the reason this trail has a five-star scenery rating.

Four decades of road work to rebuild Route 101 into a high-speed roadway were finally completed in 2005. The rail trail crosses under 101 in a long, dark culvert about a mile past the grade-level crossing of Chester Turnpike. If bicycling, you may want to dismount and walk through the culvert.

East of the culvert, Old Candia Road parallels the trail for about a mile. This was the previous Route 101 highway. Two more culverts follow where Main Street crosses the railroad grade. These are unusual for the steep hills leading up to them.

After another couple of miles, the trail comes to a large parking lot in East Candia. This location, by the Candia-Raymond border, was the site of the East Candia depot. Now it is another convenient trailhead.

From East Candia, the trail crosses power lines near the Candia-Raymond border. It then follows a small brook with open views of wetlands. The trail has a fine cinder surface here.

Suddenly you emerge by another sizable lake, Onway Lake. The site of the Onway Lake railroad stop is now owned by the Onway Lake Family Resort. Signs indicate that you should not swim at their beach.

The outlet from the lake is a small tributary of the Lamprey River. Rather than following the brook, the railroad made a small rock cut to get more directly to Raymond. Unfortunately, this cut no longer has proper drainage. As a result, you need to pick your way around the pools of standing water here.

Past the Onway Lake Road culvert, the scenery suddenly changes. Raymond's baseball and soccer playing fields appear to the north. The fields signal that you are close to Raymond Depot.

Raymond-to-Rockingham Junction Section

Like the western half of the Portsmouth Branch Trail, the eastern half has fine wetlands and pond scenery, although some sections in Epping are not so pretty. The scenery definitely improves in Newfields. The trail surface is mostly good, but there are some rough and muddy spots.

The Raymond Historical Society did a fine job restoring Raymond Depot. Take a look at their exhibits inside and the small switching locomotive, section car, caboose, and freight car outside.

Raymond Depot

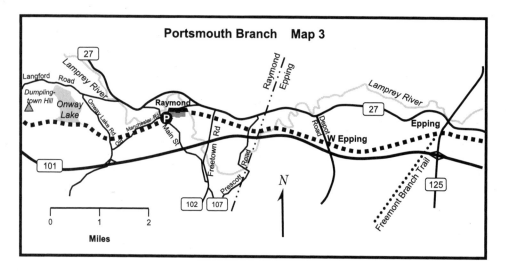

Portsmouth Branch   Map 3

27

Lamprey River

Langford Road

Dumpling-town Hill

Onway Lake

Onway Lake Rd

Old Manchester Rd

Raymond

P

Main St

Raymond

Epping

Freetown Rd

Prescott Road

102 107

101

Lamprey River

27

Depot Road

W Epping

Epping

Freemont Branch Trail

125

N

0   1   2

Miles

The trail's first crossing of the Lamprey River is close to the depot. The steel girder bridge has been used as a medium for local graffiti artists to display their talents.

The trail goes by some houses and crosses the busy Routes 102/107 highway (Freetown Road). After Prescott Road, it goes over another bridge across the Lamprey River. Stop and admire the impressive granite masonry work by the

Rockingham Depot in 2006 looked ready for renovation.

bridge. Large granite blocks fit together perfectly and look as if they could last another 150 years.

The three and a half miles between the second Lamprey River bridge and Epping feature wooded scenery with only a few road crossings. Some wetlands were green with duckweed when I scouted in late summer. A few poorly drained spots on the trail required finding a route around mud holes.

In Epping you come across the junction with the Freemont Branch Trail, the other part of the Rockingham Recreational Trail. The Portsmouth Branch Trail crosses busy Main Street and Route 125 just past the Freemont Branch Trailhead, as shown on the Epping Trailhead detail map (see trail SE7).

The woodland scenery past here changes to farm fields as you approach busy Route 27. Then, just past 27, a serene pond on the north side of the trail provides a major contrast with the NASCAR Star Speedway on the south side. If you like noisy cars, you can proceed southeast a half mile on Route 27 to check out the New England Drag Way, as well.

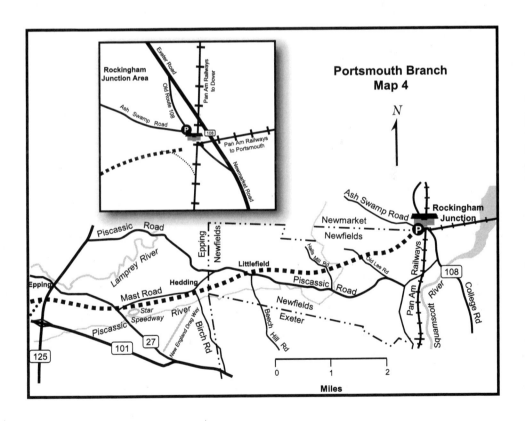

The scenery improves again past the race track, but the trail's surface becomes sandy and harder to ride on. The four final miles in Newfields are delightful, with woods, marshes, ponds, and farm fields.

Rockingham Junction is where the Portsmouth & Concord Railroad met the original Boston & Maine. The depot building still stands. It looked in bad shape in 2006 (similar to Windham Depot), but the slate roof has been kept in repair. Reportedly the building was sold in 2007, and the new owner is actively restoring it.

Eastern Railroad

Boston, MA, to Kittery, ME
Built: 1839–40
Abandoned: Salisbury, MA–Seabrook, 1982; Seabrook–Hampton, 1997
The Eastern was the first railroad to offer service between Boston and Portland.
The Eastern of New Hampshire met the Eastern of Massachusetts at Newbury-

port in 1840 and the Portland, Saco & Portsmouth Railroad at Kittery in 1842. The New Hampshire stretch was notable for its lack of construction problems, going straight through a coastal region requiring only a slight fill.

The Eastern's monopoly on Boston-to-Portland traffic soon ended, when the Boston & Maine completed a connection with the PS&P at Agamenticus in 1843. The B&M and Eastern jointly leased the PS&P in 1847, and the two railroads continued their fierce competition. Through price discounting, the B&M was able to attract the bulk of the passenger and freight traffic.

In 1870 the PS&P put itself up for sale, and the Eastern submitted the high bid. The B&M then built a competing line to Portland. Overextended, the Eastern was in poor financial shape by 1875 and finally succumbed to a B&M lease in 1885. The B&M emphasized use of its own track, gradually letting traffic wither on the Eastern and PS&P tracks.

Today there is still some freight activity on the Eastern track from Hampton north to Portsmouth. The remaining track in New Hampshire south of Hampton is unusable, with rotted ties and some missing rails.

The state purchased the right of way south of Hampton to the Massachusetts border and identified it as a potential rail trail. It is called the Hampton Branch in the May 2005 *New Hampshire State Trails Plan*, but the state has not yet committed to using it for a trail rather than for other transportation purposes. The Eastern Railroad corridor is potentially a key link in the proposed East Coast Greenway.

EAST COAST GREENWAY

The East Coast Greenway (ECG) is a proposed multi-use path that will extend from Key West, FL, to the Canadian border in Maine. This is more than a gleam in someone's eye. Work has proceeded through local efforts since 1991, and the greenway as a whole is now 20% complete. The project is gaining momentum, partly due to professional coordination from the national East Coast Greenway Alliance (www.greenway.org) based in Wakefield, Rhode Island. As of Spring 2007, a planning process was underway to identify the alignment for the greenway in New Hampshire and to build community and regional support for implementation. The state-owned portion of the Eastern Railroad right of way would be an appealing option for the ECG and hopefully can be developed as a trail in the coming years.

Proposed Hampton Branch Trail

Drakeside Road, Hampton, to Masachusetts State Line, Seabrook, 4.3 miles

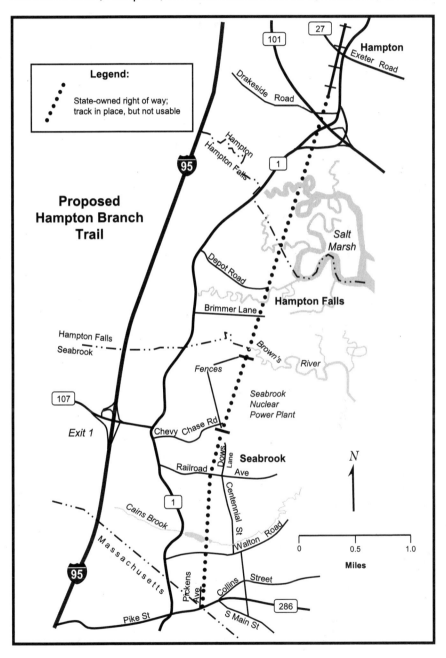

Legend:

State-owned right of way; track in place, but not usable

Hampton
Exeter Road

Drakeside Road

Proposed Hampton Branch Trail

Hampton
Hampton Falls

Salt Marsh

Depot Road

Hampton Falls

Brimmer Lane

Hampton Falls
Seabrook

Brown's River

Fences

Seabrook Nuclear Power Plant

Chevy Chase Rd

Exit 1

Railroad
Dows Lane
Seabrook
Ave

Cains Brook

Centennial St
Walton Road

Massachusetts

Pickens Ave
Collins Street

Pike St
S Main St

N

0   0.5   1.0
Miles

View of the power line service road on the railroad fill, tidal marsh, and power plant from the Route 1 North bridge

As shown on the Hampton Branch map, the proposed trail would traverse a scenic salt marsh area. There is also an intriguing Gothic arch culvert for Cairns Brook, near the southern end. However, there are major concerns. The Route 101/Route 1 intersection makes it difficult to have a northern trailhead

You can view the salt marsh from the end of Depot Road in Hampton Falls.

NEW HAMPSHIRE RAIL TRAILS

Cairns Brook overpass: they don't make culverts like this any more!

below the active Pan Am Railways track in Hampton, and the southern end goes through a poorly drained swamp. Additionally, there are security concerns about public travel near the Seabrook Nuclear Power Plant. At this time, the corridor is not open to the public.

Suncook Valley Railroad

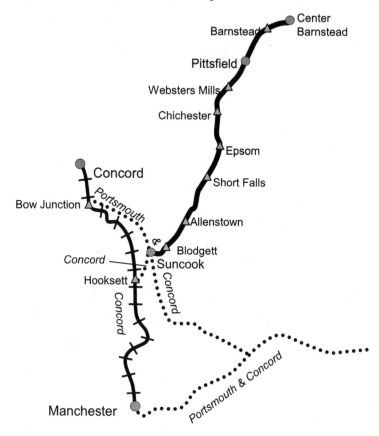

Suncook to Center Barnstead
Built: 1869
Abandoned: Pittsfield–Center Barnstead: 1947; Suncook–Pittsfield: 1953
This picturesque little railroad ran along the Suncook River through farming communities. It connected to Concord via the northern end of the Portsmouth & Concord Railroad and absorbed a short section of that track when the P&C tore up the track from Candia to Suncook. The Concord Railroad added a connection between Suncook and Hooksett.

The line was operated successively by the Concord, the Concord & Montreal, and the Boston & Maine. In 1924 it was spun off as an independent Suncook Valley Railroad again by the B&M. It operated the *Blueberry Express* train until

Missing bridge over Bear Brook

1934, and sporadic freight service continued for a couple of decades before abandonment.

Roads have taken over the right of way from Suncook to Allenstown. Much of the rest of the route is intact, but all in private ownership. It could form an excellent rail trail with local leadership, permission of the landowners, and replacement of missing bridges at Bear Brook and the Little Suncook River.

Central West Region

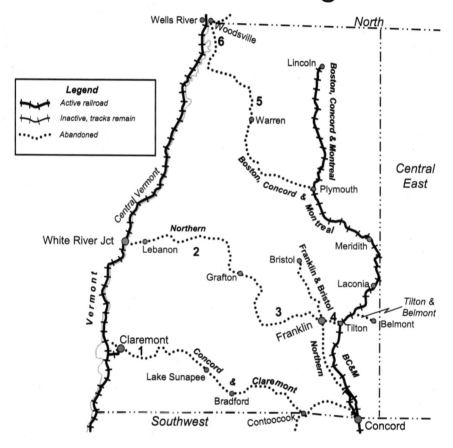

Legend
- Active railroad
- Inactive, tracks remain
- Abandoned

Wells River
Woodsville
6
Lincoln
North
Boston, Concord & Montreal
5
Warren
Boston, Concord & Montreal
Plymouth
Central Vermont
Central East
White River Jct
Northern
Lebanon
2
Meridith
Bristol
Franklin & Bristol
Grafton
Laconia
Vermont
3
Franklin
4
Tilton
Tilton & Belmont
Belmont
Claremont
1
Concord
Northern
BC&M
Lake Sunapee
&
Claremont
Bradford
Southwest
Contoocook
Concord

T HE Central West Region extends from the Connecticut River on the west to just beyond the Pemigewasset and Merrimack Rivers to the east and from Woodsville in the north down to Concord. This region contained three major New Hampshire railroads: the Concord & Claremont,

The railroads followed rivers to get through the mountains, resulting in frequent bridges like this one on the Northern in Andover.

the Northern, and the Boston, Concord & Montreal. The Franklin & Bristol had a short life as an independent line before being absorbed by the Northern. The Tilton & Belmont was a branch line for the BC&M.

All of the major lines faced the problem of how to cross a mountainous part of the state to connect the Merrimack and Connecticut river valleys. Only one line remains in service today. The route along the Pemigewasset River linking Concord with Lincoln is now owned by the state of New Hampshire and is used to service a cement plant and for tourist trains.

Concord & Claremont Railroad

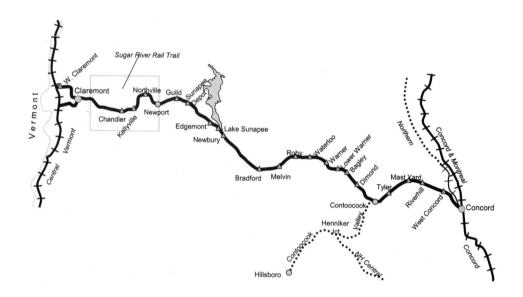

Concord to Claremont
Built: Concord–Bradford, 1848–50; Bradford–Claremont, 1870–72
Abandoned: Concord–Newport, 1960–64; Newport–Claremont, 1977

The Concord & Claremont Railroad was one of the railroad lines with lots of charm and little revenue. Built from West Concord to Bradford at the end of the 1840s, the line generated too little profit from those operations to proceed further to the intended destination of Claremont. The C&C merged with two other struggling interconnecting lines, the Contoocook Valley and the New Hampshire Central in 1853 to form the Merrimack & Connecticut Rivers Railroad. Still financially shaky, the M&CR was taken under the wing of the much more successful Northern Railroad.

Boom times following the Civil War led to a charter for the Sugar River Railroad, which inherited the challenge of building the rest of the C&C line from Bradford to Claremont. This work included the monumental task of cutting through a sizable granite rock formation just south of Newbury Harbor.

With completion of the line, the C&C became a favorite of vacationers, who would stop at Lake Sunapee Station and take a steamboat to their summer

The massive and narrow Newbury Cut just barely let a train pass through. Snow was always a problem. (Courtesy of Soo Nipi Publishing Co., Sunapee, NH)

homes or hotels on the lake. The line also carried freight from the many factories in Claremont, Newport, and Warner.

The Boston & Maine took over the C&C when it captured control of the Northern. It became their Claremont Branch. After operations withered un-

Remains of the Melvin Bridge over the Warner River (left) and Mastyard Bridge over the Contoocook (right)

der the onslaught of automobiles and trucks, the B&M sold the C&C and the Contoocook Valley lines to Samuel Pinsly in 1954.

By 1965 Pinsly had gradually abandoned the C&C all the way to Newport. He made his investment in the railroad pay off in salvage: steel from the bridges and rails and real estate. Prime Lake Sunapee waterfront fetched particularly good prices, but even the Newbury Cut stretch from Newbury to Bradford ended up in private hands.

The section from Newport to Claremont was abandoned in 1977, leaving Pinsly with a short length of track from Claremont to Claremont Junction and the B&M with a short stretch in Concord. In 1998 LaValley bought the Claremont track to ensure railroad access for their lumber supply store. Fortunately, the State of New Hampshire bought the right of way from Newport to Claremont. It is now a gem of a rail trail.

CW1. Sugar River Rail Trail

Belknap Avenue, Newport, to Claremont trailhead, 9 miles
Trail condition: ★★★ Mostly good dirt surface, but some sandy spots are treacherous for bicycling, and other spots can get muddy.
Scenery: ★★★★★ Sugar River, two covered railroad bridges, and woods; mostly away from roads.
Permitted Uses: Non-motorized travel, ATVs, and motorized trail bikes year-round, plus snowmobiles in winter.
Right of way owned by: State of New Hampshire.

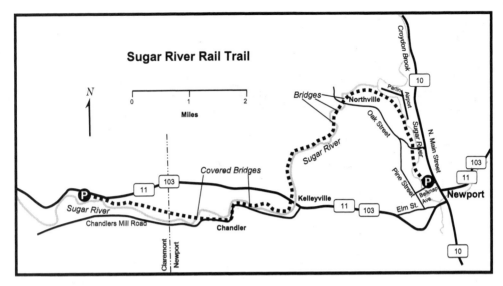

Sugar River Rail Trail

Maintained by: Trails Bureau and Shugah Valley Sno Riders.

ACCESS

There were no signs for this trail when I explored it in July 2006, so follow these instructions carefully.

The eastern trail start is off Belknap Avenue in Newport. Go a couple of blocks north of the gazebo in the center of Newport. Turn left on Belknap and take a driveway on the right just before the Johnson & Dix propane storage area. Park next to the Newport Recreational Department site.

The western end of the trail is on Routes 11/103 at the outskirts of Claremont. There is a parking lot opposite the green Claremont Self Storage facility. There is also informal parking at the 11/103 bridge across the Sugar River. It is on the north side of the highway and west side of the river. Bicyclists usually take a round trip starting and ending in Newport, about a three-hour ride.

DESCRIPTION

This is a very scenic trail with nice views of the Sugar River, interesting bridges, and remote stretches through woods. It contains two of the last five covered railroad bridges in New Hampshire. With lots of shade, the Sugar River Rail Trail makes an excellent ride on a hot summer day. ATVs and hikers are the major users, but the cinders, dirt, and sand surface works for bicycles. In some places the sand is deep enough to make difficult going and can cause a bicyclist

ATVs pass a walker. The Sugar River is to the left.

to fall. Since ATVs and trail bikes are allowed, you may have a more peaceful experience here on a weekday.

The South Branch of the Sugar River joins the main branch from Lake Sunapee in the center of Newport, but the river is still fairly small at the start of the trail on Belknap Avenue. You go over a river bridge near the start and then stay by the left bank of the Sugar River as it makes a long loop to the north. After Croydon Brook comes in from the north, the river doubles in size, but you won't see either the brook or nearby Parlin Airport due to the forest cover. Three iron bridges come in quick succession, the first just above the Oak Street crossing. Since the trail follows the river closely, you have nice views of the river and its gentle rapids all the way to Routes 11/103.

After crossing the highway, the river gradually levels off. You pass through two unusual covered bridges. The first (Pier Bridge) is over 216 feet long, as it crosses the river diagonally. Locals claim that it is the longest covered railroad bridge in the world! It is named for the masonry pier that supports the center of the span.

Past this bridge, the trail goes either very close to or on Chandlers Mill Road. It crosses the river again on the second covered bridge (Wright Bridge), and then diverges from the road.

Enlarged river bed by the bridge above Oak Street

In the final two miles to the Claremont end, the trail squeezes between Routes 11/103 and the river and finally reaches the parking lot. The river provides the scenery, and the road is shielded from sight until the end.

The city of Claremont has extended the trail beyond the parking lot up to LaValley's Building Supply. However, this is a rather unscenic stretch. It follows alongside Routes 11/103, going in front of shopping centers, until it finally veers to the left by Enterprise Rent-a-Car. You get a nice view of the river from the bridge crossing, but otherwise this extension is more for the convenience of Claremont residents than a scenic trip.

RAILROAD COVERED BRIDGES

Railroad covered bridges are extremely rare. The Claremont Branch of the B&M was one of the last to build and maintain them. As a result, three of its bridges remain: one in Contoocook and the two in Newport on the Sugar River Trail.

New Hampshire also has the "Upside Down" bridge by the Winnipesaukee River Trail and a covered bridge by Clark's Trading Post in Lincoln. Vermont has two, in Shoreham and Wolcott. Oregon has one, in Cottage Grove. That's all there are in the United States and possibly the world! Enjoy the two Sugar River bridges and consider helping to preserve them. A group in Newport is working to raise funds for restoration (see www.newportrec.com/pier-bridge.htm).

Pier Bridge with its center pier and a recently added support

Wright Bridge (left) and Contoocook Bridge (right)

Northern Railroad

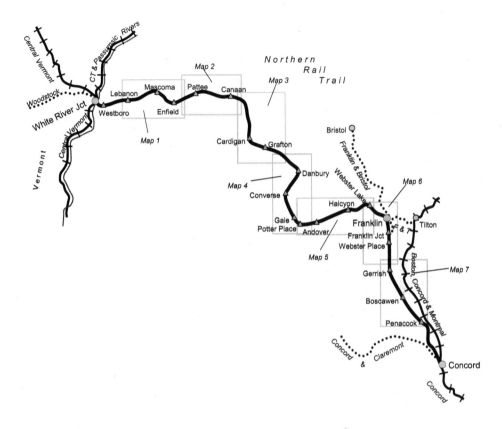

Concord to White River Jct., VT

Built: 1845–47

Abandoned: Westboro–Boscawen,1992

The Northern Railroad was one of the gorillas of New Hampshire railroads. Along with the Concord, the Boston, Concord & Montreal, and the Boston & Maine, it helped shape the history of the state's railroad industry.

Daniel Webster and his nephew, Professor Charles Haddock of Dartmouth, were primary publicists for the Northern. The railroad was incorporated and received a state charter in 1844. The biggest problem with construction was getting by the Orange Summit rock cut using the laborious manual methods of the day. Even with this obstacle, the entire sixty-mile railroad was constructed in two years in the biggest civil engineering project of its time in New Hampshire.

Shortly thereafter (June 1848), the Franklin & Bristol completed its thirteen-mile line from the Northern in Franklin along the west side of the Pemigewasset River up to Bristol. The Northern operated it for half a year and then took ownership of it.

The Northern was immediately profitable with both freight and passenger service. Financial success gave the Northern the clout to be a winner in the consolidation games. It took over the Concord & Claremont, the Contoocook Valley, and the Peterborough & Hillsborough Railroads. Under Northern control, the C&C finally reached Claremont in 1872.

The Northern didn't lose its independence until the Boston & Lowell leased the Northern and the Boston, Concord & Montreal in 1884. This action was contested by the Concord Railroad, and a New Hampshire court ruled the operation was illegal, since the Nashua & Lowell had no New Hampshire charter. When the smoke cleared, it was the Boston & Maine (which did have a New Hampshire charter) that ended up controlling all these railroads.

Names of stations on the Northern seem quaint today, as they do not match the names of the associated villages and towns. For example, the West Lebanon stop was called Westboro, the West Canaan stop was Pattee, and the East Andover stop was Halcyon. Where did these names come from? A head-on collision near East Haverhill, caused by omission of the word "East" from the train order, convinced the Boston & Maine to change the names of all stations that were the same as others except for the addition of compass directions. Most of the new names referred to prominent individuals with land or business operations near the station. Halcyon was named for a nearby island on Highland Lake.

As one of the major players, the Northern lasted longer than most in the steady twentieth-century decline of the railroads. By 1990 the B&M decided it was too costly to maintain. The state bought the entire right of way from Boscawen through Lebanon with the idea that it should be used for now as a trail; but eventually it could be a key piece of the proposed Boston-to-Montreal high-speed rail line. Guilford Transportation (who bought out the B&M) kept the section between Concord and slightly north of the Boscawen border.

The railroad removed the rails, and snowmobile clubs removed the ties, so the entire fifty-nine-mile stretch from Lebanon to south Boscawen is now usable as a snowmobile trail. Two citizens action groups have worked to make the trail usable in non-winter months. These Friends of the Northern Rail Trail are divided according to the two counties that the trail goes through, Grafton and Merrimack. The Grafton County group has created a twenty-five-mile, four-season trail from downtown Lebanon through the town of Grafton. They are working to extend the trail west as part of the Westboro rail yard redevelopment project, planning eventually to cross the Connecticut River on the railroad bridge. The Merrimack County group is developing thirty-four miles of four-season trail and has completed an initial section in Andover.

CW2. Northern Rail Trail in Grafton County

Spencer Street, Lebanon, to Grafton/Danbury border, 25 miles
Trail condition: ★ ★ ★ ★ Mostly good dirt or cinders surface, but a bit uneven. A few previously unpleasant ballast rock stretches were improved with bluestone hardpack in 2007.
Scenery: ★ ★ ★ ★ ★ Rivers and lakes, views of Cardigan Mountain, varied terrain, two depot buildings.
Permitted uses: Non-motorized travel year-round; snowmobiles, ATVs, and motorized trail bikes in winter when snow-covered.
Right of way owned by: State of New Hampshire.
Maintained by: Trails Bureau, Friends of the Northern Rail Trail in Grafton County, Twin State Trailbusters, and Mt. Cardigan Snowmobile Club.

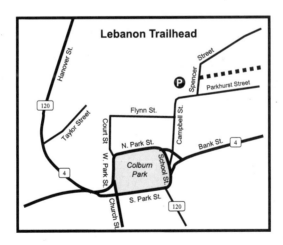

ACCESS
For the Lebanon trailhead, take Exit 18 off of I-89 and head south on Route 120, as shown on the Lebanon Trailhead map. Go around Colburn Park and

The trail gives you outstanding views of Mascoma Lake.

head north on Campbell Street. A quick right on Parkhurst Street and left on Spencer, and you'll see the trailhead on your right. Park in the town lot opposite the trailhead or where you can find a spot near Colburn Park.

The town of Enfield has a new rail trail parking area in downtown Enfield, near the intersection of Shaker Hill and Main Street, close to the depot. You

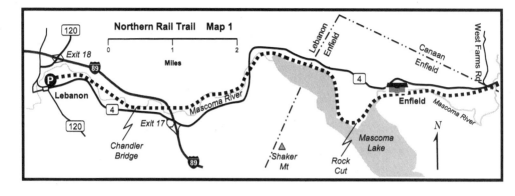

New Hampshire Rail Trails

can easily miss it when driving through Enfield on Route 4. As shown on the Enfield Detail map, take Main Street or Shaker Hill Road south from Route 4, and you'll see the new trail parking area.

At the southern end, there is good trail access, parking, and a picnic area at Sargent Hill Road in Grafton, just off Route 4.

DESCRIPTION

This trail follows the Mascoma and Indian Rivers, with an amazing twenty bridges in less than twenty-five miles up to the divide at the Orange Summit.

Heading from the Lebanon trailhead, you climb along the Mascoma River. There are frequent river crossings—nine bridges in the four miles before you reach Mascoma Lake. These are all steel I-beam construction, as the Boston & Maine had to replace the old wooden bridges to hold the weight of heavier, more powerful locomotives.

The fourth bridge from the trailhead is Chandler Bridge, made notorious by the famous wreck of 1886. Just beyond this bridge, Riverside Drive comes close to the trail and then crosses it, as shown on the Chandler Bridge Area map. If you backtrack west on Riverside Drive, you can see the nicely restored Packard Hill Covered Bridge.

Returning to the trail, you cross under the interstate highway after the fifth bridge and then cruise by the river, getting frequent views of this class II-III spring whitewater stream. In the summer it is a trickle over a gravel base.

For over two miles, the trail then gives you wonderful views of Mascoma Lake as you pass along its northern edge. Originally, the railroad surveyors preferred a route south of the lake. The existing route, requiring a substantial

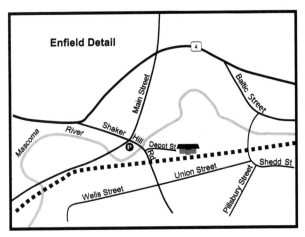

THE CHANDLER BRIDGE WRECK OF 1886

An equipment inventory in June 1884 mentioned that the 124-foot Chandler Bridge span "tended to swing sideways and should be replaced soon." However, nothing was done about replacing or shoring it up until the locomotive **Atlantic** came through with a freight load on April 30, 1886. The engineer proceeded slowly, but felt the bridge giving way, so he went full throttle. The locomotive got to the other side just as the bridge collapsed with the rest of the train. Apparently nobody was injured, and the engineer's alert action saved the **Atlantic.**

(Courtesy of the Leavitt Collection, Lebanon Historical Society)

Rock cut by Mascoma Lake

rock cut, was chosen in order to leave the Shaker settlements and farmland on the other side intact. Supposedly the Shakers donated land for the railroad on the north side in return for the promise that all passenger trains would stop at Enfield.

Near the end of the lake stretch, you come through an impressive rock cut. Although about the same height as the Orange Summit cut, it is much shorter

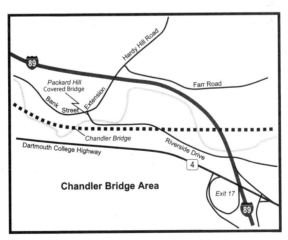

The Mascoma bridges have been decked for bicycle, pedestrian, and snowmobile use.

and did not slow down the construction as badly. Beyond the lake you pass the nicely restored Enfield depot.

After entering Canaan near the first Blackwater Road crossing, you come to five more Mascoma River bridges before the river diverts north and you pick up its Indian River tributary. From here the railroad and Route 4 took roughly the same path all the way to Andover center.

Heading east along the Indian River, the trail crosses four more bridges on its way to Mirror Lake. The Potato Road crossing marks the start of a mile in which the terrain is very flat and the trail is so close to Route 4 it feels like a sidewalk. However, the pastoral scenery to the south softens the impression of this section.

The terrain changes abruptly where the trail crosses under Grist Hill Road in a culvert. Under the road bridge across the Indian River, the stream drops precipitously in a scenic rapid that you should check out.

After you pass the freight house where the railroad had its Canaan stop, you climb up to a culvert under Route 4 and then come to an exceptionally pretty spot: Mirror Lake. Cardigan Mountain rises majestically in the background.

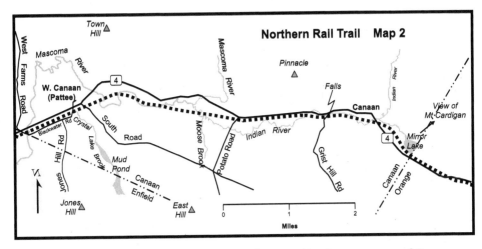

At the end of Mirror Lake, you cross the town line into a corner of Orange. The trail only goes a short distance through Orange, but it includes the infamous Orange Summit, the high point (770 feet) on the Northern Rail Trail.

South of the Orange Summit, you start down the Smith River. The trail passes two more ponds, Tewksbury Pond and Kilton Pond, and then goes through Grafton Center. Grafton had a large granite quarry. Also, the Ruggles Mine, a mica, feldspar, beryl, and uranium mine, is a short side trip west on Riddle Hill Road; it is open to the public for a fee. (See www.RugglesMine.com.)

The Smith River drops very little as it meanders through Grafton. This is surprisingly different from the stretch further downstream along Route 104, where it plunges through the mountains to reach the Pemigewasset River.

Mirror Lake and Cardigan Mountain—a great picnic spot!

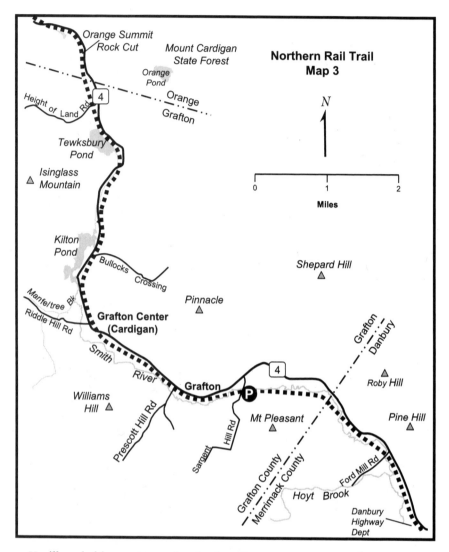

You'll probably want to end a Grafton County excursion at the picnic spot and trail access area by Sargent Hill Road. You may proceed across the county line as far as the Danbury Highway Department site (Map 4, next trail description) before getting stopped by continuous heavy ballast rock. However, the Highway Department does not want a lot of cars parked at their facility, and you should ask permission before leaving your car there.

ORANGE SUMMIT ROCK CUT

This forty-foot-deep cut enabled the railroad to take a shorter, easier path. However, the cut itself was brutal, requiring months of hand drilling and blasting. It was supposed to be simplified by the presence of a peat bog in the middle, but that too was problematic. Ooze kept seeping back into the cut, and the construction crew finally had to burn off the peat.

The railroad needed to complete construction to Lebanon quickly in order to generate revenue. With the rock cut proceeding so slowly, the engineers decided to portage a locomotive around it. Supposedly they used the highway (built in the early 1800s), a team of oxen, and probably a good deal of rope. One wonders how they actually accomplished this feat, especially considering the steep highway grade. They were successful, however, and the track was laid down quickly to Lebanon.

The Orange Summit rock cut was an impressive feat for 1846.

Northern Rail Trail in Merrimack County: Proposed Trail North of Potter Place

Grafton/Danbury town line to Potter Place, Andover, 11 miles

In the 1950s the Boston & Maine upgraded the railroad bed from Concord to the Danbury Highway Department by bringing in ballast rock as a base for the ties and track. The ballast provided excellent drainage and stabilized the right of way; but now that the rails and ties are gone, the ballast remains as the trail surface. It is extremely difficult to walk or bicycle upon, so it makes the trail virtually unusable when not snow-covered.

The primary goal of the Friends of the Northern Rail Trail in Merrimack County is to replace the ballast rock with a hardpack surface similar in composition to a dirt road or driveway. The Friends have obtained a federal Transportation Enhancement Grant for this stretch, but the money will not be available until 2010.

The initial 2¼-mile section from the county border to the Danbury Highway Department site serves as a continuation of the Grafton County trail. It has a good hardpack surface and follows the Smith River away from the highway.

The ballast rock south of the Danbury Highway Department site is unpleasant to ride or walk on.

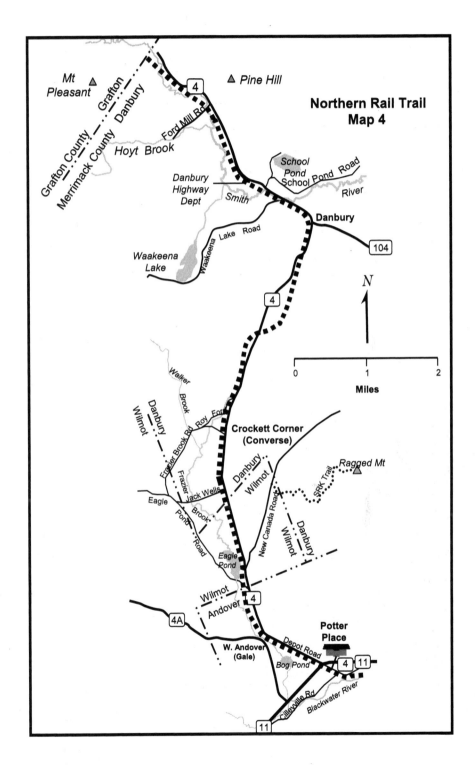

Northern Rail Trail
Map 4

Mt Pleasant

Pine Hill

Grafton County

Grafton

Danbury

Merrimack County

Ford Mill Rd

Hoyt Brook

School Pond

School Pond Road

River

Danbury Highway Dept

Smith

Danbury

104

Waakeena Lake Road

Waakeena Lake

4

N

0   1   2
Miles

Walker

Brook

Danbury

Wilmot

Roy Ford

Crockett Corner
(Converse)

Ragged Mt

SRK Trail

Frazier Brook Rd

Frazier

Jack Wells

Danbury

Wilmot

Eagle

Brook

New Canada Road

Danbury

Wilmot

Pond

Road

Eagle Pond

Wilmot

Andover

4

4A

Potter Place

W. Andover
(Gale)

Depot Road

Bog Pond

4 11

Cilleyville Rd

Blackwater River

11

Winter view of Eagle Pond from the trail

At the Highway Department, non-winter travel comes to a halt because of the ballast rock. However, with enough snow, there is no problem taking a snowmobile or cross country skis. After 2010 the trail should be in fine shape for four-season use.

Attractions on this stretch include the center of Danbury, Frazier Brook, and Eagle Pond. Danbury is a classic New Hampshire village that looks as if it has changed little since the heyday of the railroad.

The southern end of this stretch of trail is Potter Place, where the Northern Rail Trail becomes an excellent four-season trail.

CW3. Northern Rail Trail in Merrimack County: Andover 4-Season Trail

Potter Place, Andover, to Maple Street, East Andover 5.7 miles.
Trail condition: ★ ★ ★ ★ ★ Recently applied hardpack makes a great dirt trail surface.
Scenery: ★ ★ ★ ★ ★ Andover Historical Society buildings at Potter Place, Blackwater River, a covered bridge, Horseshoe Pond, Highland Lake, and views of Mount Kearsarge.

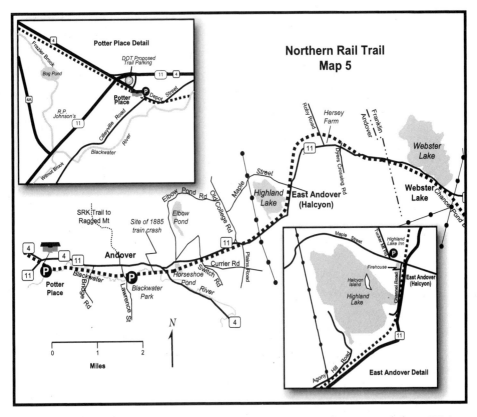

Northern Rail Trail Map 5

Potter Place Detail

East Andover Detail

Permitted uses: Non-motorized travel year-round; snowmobiles, ATVs, and motorized trail bikes in winter when snow-covered.

Right of way owned by: State of New Hampshire.

Maintained by: Trails Bureau, Friends of the Northern Rail Trail in Merrimack County, and the Andover Snowmobile Club.

ACCESS

To reach Potter Place on the west end of the trail, exit Route 11 to the south at the interchange with Route 4. You'll see the Potter Place depot and caboose. Limited parking is available by the freight house or across the street, compliments of the Andover Historical Society. The New Hampshire Department of Transportation proposes to construct true trail parking as part of the project to replace the current Route 11 bridge over Route 4 at Potter Place.

This section of trail, near town and already upgraded with a good hardpack surface, is well used. (Peter Southworth)

For access from Blackwater Park, take Lawrence Street south from Route 11 in the center of Andover. After crossing the Blackwater River, the small park will be on your left. The trail is beside the parking area.

At East Andover, you can access the trail from Channel Road, between the lake and the trail. Limited parking is available off of Channel Road. More parking is available at the Trail Welcome Center at Highland Lake Inn, 32 Maple Street, at the intersection of Tucker Mountain Road.

DESCRIPTION

This stretch of the Northern Rail Trail has a lot to look at and a great trail surface. The Andover Elementary/Middle School and the town's Blackwater Park are in the center, so the trail gets a lot of use.

Construction of a four-season trail is an ongoing project of the Friends of the Northern Rail Trail in Merrimack County. The group started with the Potter Place-to-Blackwater Park stretch in 2005. Work in 2006 brought the trail to Switch Road and in 2007 to Maple Street, making 5.7 miles of trail in all. If the group receives an additional Recreational Trails Program Grant in 2008, the trail will be extended at least to the Andover/Franklin town line. Continuation in 2009 will bring it to Webster Lake in Franklin.

The trail-building effort requires grading off most of the ballast rock and replacing it with scores of truckloads of hardpack material. The work in 2007 required 127 truckloads, over 2500 tons. A grader spreads the material to the appropriate width and depth, and a roller compacts it into a hard surface.

This work has relied on extensive volunteer labor and equipment, provided by the Friends group and Andover Snowmobile Club personnel. However, the hardpack material is costly in the quantity required. Recreational Trail Program (RTP) funds from the New Hampshire Bureau of Trails have been critical for obtaining it.

Here is what you'll see on the finished part of the trail, starting at Potter Place and traveling east:

In the railroad's heyday, Potter Place was a busy station with a major hotel. Stage coaches regularly took passengers from there to Wilmot and New

The trail crosses Bridge Road at this picturesque covered bridge next to the railroad bridge over the Blackwater River.

*Vacationers traveled in style on a Concord
Coach from Potter Place to New London.
(Courtesy of the Andover Historical Society)*

London. Thanks to the Andover Historical Society, you can still admire some of the Potter Place facilities, including the restored depot, freight house, and general store.

The Blackwater River starts at R. P. Johnson's building supply on Route 11 where Frazier Brook and Wilmot Brook merge. Moving east from Potter Place, you stay close to the meandering Blackwater until it turns south near the trail crossing of Route 4. The first bridge, about a half mile from Potter Place, comes

The Andover Crash of 1885

October 18, 1885, was a foggy day with poor visibility. A freight train headed by the locomotive **Northern** stopped at East Andover and proceeded west. At West Andover, it was discovered that eight freight cars had come lose at East Andover, so the **Northern** went back to fetch them. Meanwhile an express passenger train led by the engine **Kearsarge** came to West Andover and was advised that the freight would be waiting at East Andover for the express to pass.

Apparently there was a misunderstanding, with the engineer on the **Northern** expecting the **Kearsarge** to wait briefly at West Andover. As a result, the two trains were going top speed in the fog when they collided three-fifths of a mile east of Andover Center. The engines were demolished, three crew members were killed, and five others were injured in the wreck.

at the foot of a gentle rapid. The second railroad bridge is right next to the covered bridge on Bridge Road. The view upstream from the center of the covered bridge is one of my favorites.

After another mile, you cross Lawrence Street through a culvert and emerge at Blackwater Park, a small ball field. Efforts are underway to construct toilet facilities there. A third of a mile past Blackwater Park, you get to the site one of the Northern's worst train crashes.

Halcyon (East Andover) Station. The church and bridge are still here, but the tracks are gone and the station was replaced by a firehouse.
(Courtesy of the Andover Historical Society)

You then cross a small truss bridge, marked on both sides by "telltales." These are horizontal bars holding a set of vertical metal strips that hang down toward the track. If a train worker were on one of the cars and couldn't see the bridge coming, then a telltale would tickle his back, reminding him to keep down.

You go under the Route 4 bridge and then come to Horseshoe Pond. It was divided into two ponds by the causeway created for the railroad. Beyond Switch Road, the trail follows Route 11 very closely and crosses it at Plains Road. Then it proceeds by beautiful Highland Lake and the quaint East Andover (Halcyon) village. The East Andover trailhead is at Channel Road, just south of the firehouse that was built on the site of the Halcyon Depot.

The Highland Lake Inn at 32 Maple Street in East Andover is pioneering the concept of Trail Welcome Centers at inns on the trail. The welcome center provides information about the trail, restroom facilities, simple snacks and drinks for sale, and parking.

Wetlands between Horseshoe Pond and Switch Road

Mount Kearsarge rises over cornfields along the trail.

New Hampshire Rail Trails

Northern Rail Trail in Merrimack County: Proposed Trail South of Andover

Maple Street, East Andover, to start of track, Boscawen, 19 miles

This nineteen-mile section of the trail is a major challenge due to the length needing construction of a four-season hardpack surface. At an estimated cost of $20,000 per mile, this will require an investment of approximately $400,000. Unless a generous benefactor appears, the most likely source of funds of this magnitude is a federal Transportation Enhancement grant. The Friends group is working to rally support in Franklin and Boscawen to make this improvement happen and is also chipping away at the problem with small projects each year moving east from Andover.

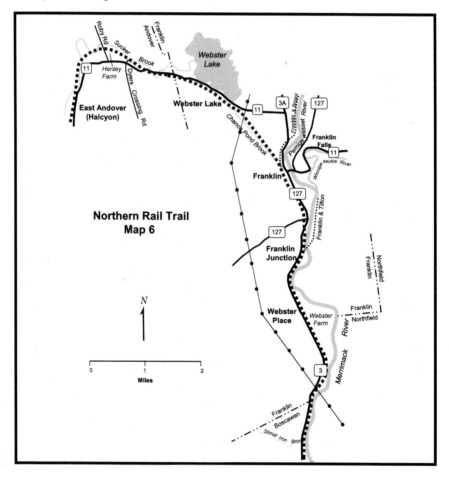

Ballast and hardpack before and after Andover 4-Season Trail construction

Again, this section is easily accessible by snowmobile riders or cross country skiers in the winter, although unusable the rest of the year. Some major attractions are Sucker Brook (the outlet of Highland Lake), the Hersey Farm, Webster Lake, and the Merrimack River.

Bridge abutments are all that remain of the Franklin & Tilton Railroad's crossing of the Merrimack near Franklin Junction. The Winnipesaukee River Trail Association is working to make a trail connection through Franklin between their trail along the Winnipesaukee River and the Northern Rail Trail.

The Gerrish depot is a candidate for restoration.

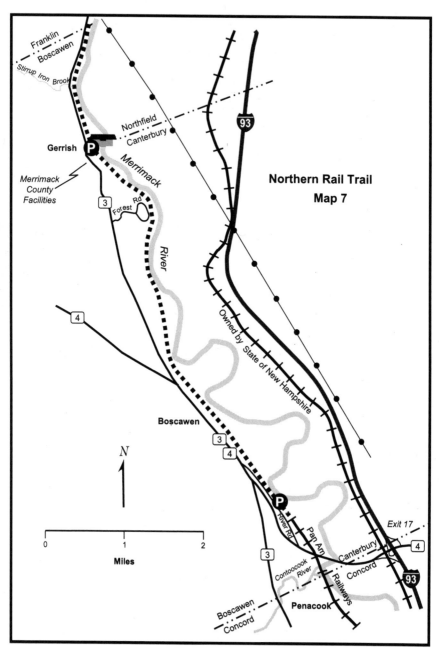

Northern Rail Trail

Map 7

Franklin
Boscawen

Stirrup Iron Brook

Northfield
Canterbury

93

Gerrish P

Merrimack

Merrimack
County
Facilities

3

Forest Rd

River

4

Owned by State of New Hampshire

Boscawen

N

3

4

P

0   1   2

Miles

River Rd

Pan Am

Exit 17

4

3

Canterbury

Concord

Railways

93

Contoocook
River

Boscawen
Concord

Penacook

Further south, the Daniel Webster Farm is the site of ongoing preservation effort by the Webster Farm Preservation Association and the Trust for Public Land. It will be a major destination for users when the trail is improved.

The scenic stretch south of Gerrish has excellent views of the Merrimack River.

There is a convenient parking area at Gerrish Depot, just north of the Merrimack County facilities. South of Gerrish, there are about three and a half particularly scenic miles of trail away from the road and often very close to a placid stretch of the Merrimack River.

The last two miles along Routes 3 and 4 are a bit of an anticlimax at this time, as there is no real destination. The state-owned right of way ends where the Pan Am Railways tracks stop in the middle of a farm field in Boscawen.

Ultimately, the Northern Rail Trail should extend down into Concord. This could possibly be done with a "rail with trail" configuration or using some of the existing Concord trails near the track.

Franklin & Bristol Railroad

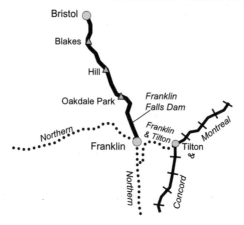

Franklin to Bristol
Built: 1847–48
Abandoned: North of Franklin Falls Dam, 1937; south of dam, 1940.

This short spur line was completed just after the Northern Railroad; it linked Bristol with the Northern at Franklin. It was operated first by the Northern Railroad and then by the Boston & Maine. Through much of its life, this line carried four passenger trains daily, as well as freight traffic.

Floods in March of 1936 washed away sections of the railroad grade, at which point the B&M abandoned regular train service. However, the southern end of the line was used to help build the massive Franklin Falls flood control dam, and then the whole railroad was abandoned.

The entire stretch from the Franklin Falls Dam to Bristol is now in the flood plain behind the dam. Since the Pemigewasset River only backs up here during severe flooding, the land is usually dry. The railroad grade is either missing or totally overgrown in many stretches, but the old Route 3 location by the river is a marvelous place to bicycle, ski, or snowmobile. You can see where the town of Hill was before all its inhabitants were moved and its buildings taken down.

South of the dam, the right of way still exists and provides views of the Pemigewasset River. Although privately owned, it could become a connecting trail between the Northern Rail Trail and the Franklin Falls flood plain.

The last stretch to the junction with the Northern Railroad will probably be useful as part of the connection yet to be made between the Winnipesaukee River Trail and the Northern Rail Trail.

Boston, Concord & Montreal Railroad

Concord to Lincoln and Woodsville

Built: Concord–Plymouth, 1849–50; Plymouth–Woodsville/Wells River, VT, 1850–53; Plymouth–Lincoln, 1880–94, Tilton–Belmont, 1889; Franklin–Tilton, 1892.

The Winnipesaukee Scenic Railroad train at Weirs Beach.

Abandoned: Tilton–Belmont, 1934; Franklin Jct.–Franklin Falls, 1942; Plymouth–Blackmount, 1954; Franklin Falls–Tilton, 1975; Blackmount–Woodsville, 1981.

New Hampshire granted the Boston, Concord & Montreal Railroad a charter in 1844. As its name suggests, the intent was to link Boston with Montreal via Concord. Initial construction from 1849 to 1853 built the line from Concord to the Connecticut River, going through Plymouth, Warren, and Woodsville. In Woodsville it connected with the White Mountains Railroad and the railroad bridge over the Connecticut River to Wells River, VT.

The BC&M expanded by lease, acquisition, and construction. It operated the White Mountains line from 1853 and the Pemigewasset Valley Railroad, running from Plymouth to Woodstock, from its construction in 1883. The PV was extended to Lincoln with help from lumber baron J. E. Henry, who needed a connection for his East Branch & Lincoln Railroad. However, it never went beyond Lincoln through Franconia Notch.

In its drive to dominate New England railroads, the Boston & Lowell Railroad leased the BC&M in 1884. After the Concord Railroad strenuously objected, the New Hampshire Supreme Court ruled this arrangement to be illegal, since the B&L lacked a New Hampshire charter. The BC&M and the Concord then joined forces to form the Concord & Montreal Railroad in 1889.

The new railroad expanded with two small branch lines, the Franklin & Tilton and Tilton & Belmont, and also acquired a significant amount of Lake Shore Railroad stock. The Boston & Maine acquired the overextended C&M in 1895.

In the twentieth century, the branch lines were abandoned first, followed by the Plymouth-to-Woodsville line. The B&M's successor, Guilford Transportation Industries, could not make money on the remaining track and sold it to the State of New Hampshire in 1974. The state's Department of Transportation is working hard to keep tourist trains running through this scenic stretch in the Lakes Region. Currently, the Hobo and Winnipesaukee Railroads operate antique diesel locomotive trains between Meredith and Lakeport during the summer and up to Plymouth for summer and fall excursions. Many of their antique railroad cars are stored in Northfield near the current end of the Winnipesaukee River Trail.

CW4. Winnipesaukee River Trail

Trestle View Park, Franklin, to Park Street, Northfield, 3.1 miles
Trail condition: ★★★★ Excellent hardpack surface most of the way, but problems with erosion near the trail start.
Scenery: ★★★★★ Rapids on the Winnipesaukee River, two impressive railroad bridges, a beautiful park at the trailhead, antique rail cars, and the Tilton depot.
Permitted uses: Non-motorized travel only.
Right of way owned by: State of New Hampshire and private landowners who have given easements for the trail.
Maintained by: Winnipesaukee River Trail Association.

ACCESS

The western end of the trail is the handsome new Trestle View Park, marked by a huge iron flywheel, on the north side of Routes 3 and 11 in the heart of Franklin. After parking there, cross the busy highway and pick up the trail on the south side of the trestle bridge.

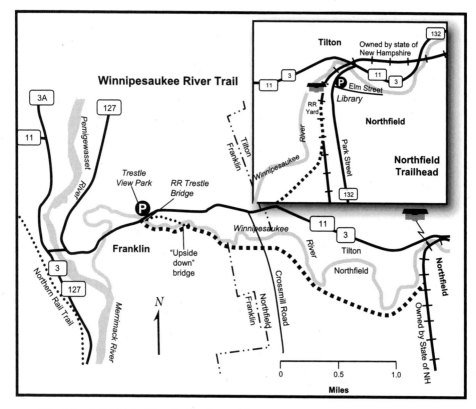

Winnipesaukee River Trail

The Northfield Trailhead detail map shows the access to the eastern end of the trail. You can park in the Northfield Public Library lot across Elm Street from the library. The trail starts south of the Northfield-Tilton depot.

DESCRIPTION

This trail is a terrific example of what a dedicated citizens action committee can accomplish. The Winnipesaukee River Trail Association (WRTA) developed both the Trestle View Park in Franklin and the three-mile trail from Franklin to Northfield, using much of the Franklin & Tilton Branch corridor.

The land for the park was a generous gift of Bob and Andrea Grevior, who own the furniture store next door. The park was designed to be a convenient take-out for kayakers running the rapids you see from the trail.

Going upstream from the park, you pass the trestle bridge and travel along the steep south bank of the river. Ideally, the trail would have taken the old railroad grade on the north side, using the two railroad bridges. However, the cost of renovating the bridges to be safe for trail users was prohibitive. Hence,

The impressive trestle at the start of the trail stands over an exciting rapid for kayakers.

the WRTA had to get easements from numerous landowners to achieve passage on the south side.

This route is steep at the start and suffered erosion in the heavy rains during the fall of 2005 and spring of 2006. The WRTA plans to fix this by paving the most problematic sections.

You soon come to a side path to the second railroad bridge. Franklin residents call it the "Upside Down" bridge, because it was a covered railroad bridge with the tracks on top. The roof was made of sheets of metal that overlap like shingles. Much of the bridge was charred by a fire, so it is not safe to walk on.

The Winnipesaukee River has major rapids all the way from Trestle View Park to Crossmill Road (where the kayakers start). Above Crossmill, it flattens out and you pass by a meandering stream.

Near the eastern end of the trail, you come to the Concord-to-Plymouth tracks owned by the state of New Hampshire. The Winnipesaukee and Hobo Railroads occasionally use them to move their antique train cars. At this time, the trail ends rather abruptly at Park Street in Northfield, where the scenic railroads store cars. The Northfield-Tilton depot (located on the Northfield side of the Winnipesaukee River) is here by the train yard.

Winnipesaukee Trail

The Lakes Region Planning Commission has had a dream for years to construct a scenic trail along the Winnipesaukee River and Lake Winnipesaukee going all the way from Franklin to Meredith. Much of this trail would use the still active Boston, Concord & Montreal Railroad right of way. The biggest problems with "rail with trail" projects are safety considerations and locating a trail beside the track along a narrow railroad grade.

In 1997 a kickoff meeting of interested parties decided that the best approach to make the trail dream a reality was to divide the overall project into short sections, with a citizens action committee responsible for each section. The trail sections are: Winnipesaukee River (Franklin, Tilton, and Northfield), Belmont, Winnisquam–Opechee–Winnipesaukee (WOW) in Laconia, and Meredith. The first three have secured federal grants, but still have extensive planning hurdles to overcome. The Meredith group only formed recently.

The overall trail concept includes a boat cruise across the lake from Weirs Beach to Wolfeboro, which will provide access to the Cotton Valley Trail on the old Wolfeboro Railroad line.

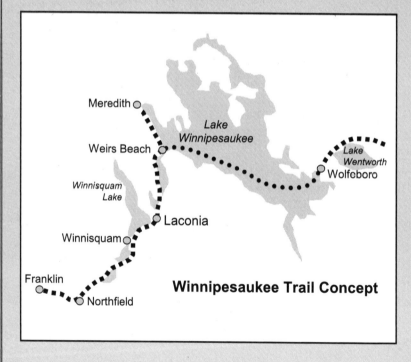

Winnipesaukee Trail Concept

The "Upside Down" bridge has a roof of metal shingles with the track on top.

The WRTA is working to extend the trail using a combination of parkland and rail-with-trail stretches as part of the overall Winnipesaukee Trail concept.

CW5. Warren Recreational Trail

Village Green, Warren, to Route 25, Benton, 6 miles
Trail condition: ★ ★ ★ ★ Level dirt surface.
Scenery: ★ ★ ★ ★ In the woods away from roads most of the way, views of Mount Moosilauke to the northeast.
Permitted uses: Non-motorized travel plus snowmobiles, ATVs, and trail bikes. OHRVs are allowed year-round.
Right of way owned by: State of New Hampshire for first four miles; then Oliverian School and other private landowners.
Maintained by: Trails Bureau and Asquamchumauke Valley Snowmobile Club.

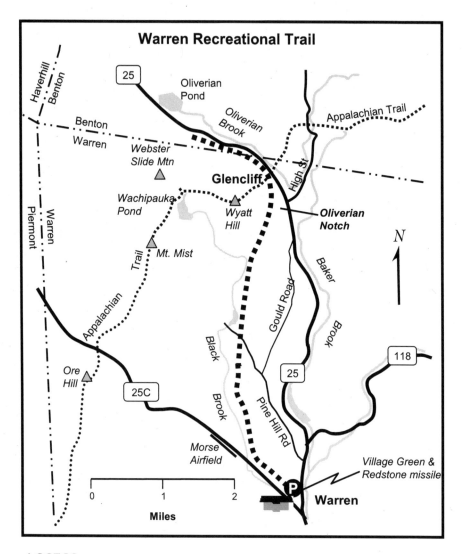

ACCESS

On the south end, park at the village green in Warren, marked strangely by an upright Redstone missile that dominates the scene. The village green was originally a railroad yard. The Warren depot is now the Mousilaukee Medical Center.

On the north end, the trail ends up at Route 25, near the Warren-Benton line, but that is not a good trailhead, and there is no parking. You should plan to make a round trip from Warren. Pine Hill Road crosses the trail about two and a half miles north from the Warren village green, but there is no parking.

The Redstone missile in Warren marks the start of the trail.

DESCRIPTION

This is a surprisingly pretty stretch of trail through a seldom visited part of New Hampshire. It goes through Oliverian Notch, a gentle pass between the south-flowing Baker Brook and the northwest-flowing Oliverian Brook. Route 25 follows Baker Brook, whereas the railroad grade followed Black Brook, so the trail is about a mile away from the highway for most of the distance.

Starting at the missile, the trail heads north along Black Brook. It is mostly a trail through the woods, with a pleasant stream nearby. After crossing Pine Hill Road, a beaver pond on the brook opens up a view of the hills to the west. Then the trail passes through a rock cut.

Oliverian Notch is so flat that it's hard to tell you have reached a pass. The only sign of the Glencliff station area is a red house near the trail. Even the Appalachian Trail passes so stealthily that you have to be looking for it to spot it. From here the Appalachian Trail goes northeast to the summit of Mount Moosilauke.

For the last mile, the trail comes close to Route 25, and then it is cut off by the highway. Apparently creation of Oliverian Pond required moving the high-

Mount Mist and the beaver pond on Black Brook

way so that it took over a stretch of the railroad grade. The right of way exists beyond the pond but is owned by East Haverhill Academy, and the school does not allow the public to use it.

West of East Haverhill, there are missing bridges, and the right of way is cut up by private property. However, there is a good trail (CW6, see below) starting just beyond the site of the Blackmount Depot.

CW6. North Haverhill–Woodsville Trail

Clark Pond Road, North Haverhill, to Route 302, Woodsville, 3.6 miles
Trail condition: ★ ★ ★ ★ Level dirt.
Scenery: ★ ★ ★ Views of farms, hills, and Connecticut River, tempered by clutter and close contact with Route 10.
Permitted uses: Non-motorized travel plus snowmobiles.
Right of way owned by: Unknown, but this section of the railroad right of way is heavily used.
Maintained by: Unknown.

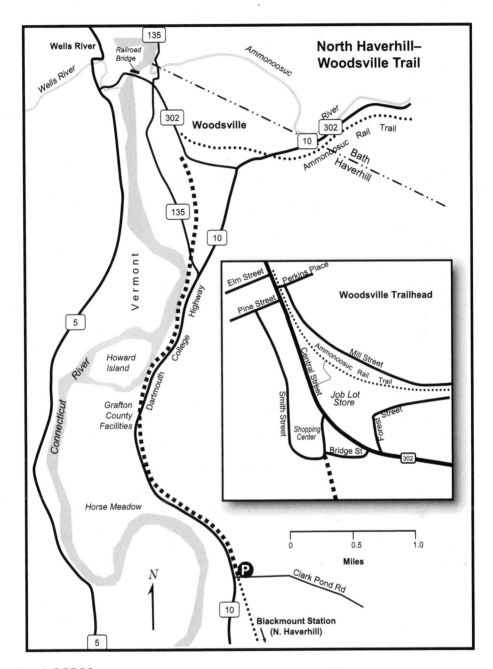

Map labels:

Wells River · 135 · Railroad Bridge · Ammonoosuc · North Haverhill–Woodsville Trail · Wells River · 302 · Woodsville · River · 302 · Trail · 10 · Ammonoosuc Rail · Bath · Haverhill · 135 · 10 · Vermont · 5 · Highway · College · Dartmouth · Howard Island · Connecticut · River · Grafton County Facilities · Horse Meadow · N · P · Clark Pond Rd · 10 · Blackmount Station (N. Haverhill) · 5

Inset: Woodsville Trailhead · Elm Street · Perkins Place · Pine Street · Central Street · Mill Street · Ammonoosuc Rail Trail · Job Lot Store · Smith Street · Forest Street · Shopping Center · Bridge St · 302

Scale: 0 · 0.5 · 1.0 · Miles

ACCESS

The North Haverhill access is straightforward. Take Route 10 to Clark Pond Road, which is near a Mobil station. Clark Pond Road immediately crosses the

Farm with Mount Moosilauke in the background

railroad right of way. There is room for several cars to park off the road there.

The Woodsville end is harder to find. You should be able to find a parking spot at the Ocean State Job Lot store on Route 302 (Central Street) or at the small shopping center on the other side of the highway. The trailhead is by the intersection of Smith and Bridge Street, shown on the Woodsville Trailhead detail map. An informal path on the side of the Job Lot parking lot connects to the Ammonoosuc Recreational Trail (N1).

DESCRIPTION

This trail exhibits a mixture of very pretty views and junk, so it was difficult to rate for scenery. Given its short distance, I wouldn't expect anyone to travel far for the experience, particularly with the spectacular Ammonoosuc Recreational Trail close by. Still, you may want to try it to get a much nicer view of the Connecticut River than the one from the Fort Hill Trail (SW2) and to see a couple of classic farms with Mount Moosilauke in the background.

Starting at Clark Pond Road, you soon come to the large farms with views of mountains to the southeast. Then you come to a stretch where the railroad grade became a driveway for several houses. You stay close to Route 10 until crossing over it at the Grafton County complex. Although you are still close to the highway, there is enough separation to make this the scenic highlight of the walk or ride. For almost a mile, you closely follow a placid stretch of the Connecticut River. The river and farm fields on the floodplain provide open views of the hills to the west.

You then cross over Route 135 and make your way to the Woodsville trailhead. The trail stops rather abruptly at Smith Street, making one wonder, "Where did the railroad go?" If you continue along Smith Street to Route 302, cross the highway, and take the informal path up from the Job Lot store to the Ammonoosuc Trail, you'll find the junction of the Boston, Concord & Montreal and White Mountains Railroad rights of way.

Trail by the Connecticut River

Central East Region

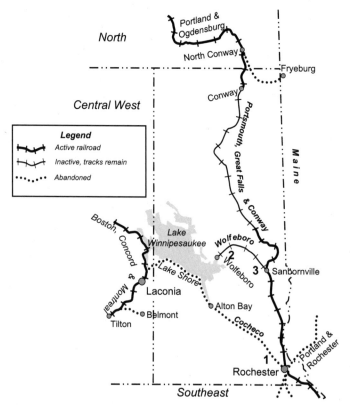

THE Central East Region extends from Lake Winnipesaukee in the west to the Maine border in the east and from North Conway in the north down to Rochester.

This small region included four New Hampshire railroads: the Lake Shore; Cochecho; Wolfeboro; and Portsmouth, Great Falls & Conway. Although these

Abandoned tracks in place, with trail alongside or between the rails, are common in this region, as on this short stretch of the Wolfeboro Branch Recreational Trail in Wakefield (CE3).

lines covered a lot of miles through interesting lake and mountain scenery, the region has few good rail trails.

The Lake Shore Railroad had a short life devoted primarily to passenger traffic for vacationers going to Lake Winnipesaukee. Abandoned over seventy years ago, little remains for trail use. The Cochecho right of way has been carved up among private owners for most of its distance, although there is a state-owned trail from Farmington to Rochester. The Wolfeboro Railroad right of way became a multi-use rail trail for hiking, bicycling, and running antique section cars over the track. Railroad maintenance personnel used these self-propelled vehicles (also called speeder cars or putt putts) to check the condition of the track and bridges.

The Portsmouth, Great Falls & Conway is still an active rail corridor between Conway and North Conway and between southern Ossipee and the junction with the Boston & Maine's original line near Dover. In the middle, the state owns a twenty-one-mile stretch from the Conway border to southern Ossipee. The track is still in place, so this stretch is only usable as a trail in the winter when snow covers the ties and rails.

Cochecho Railroad

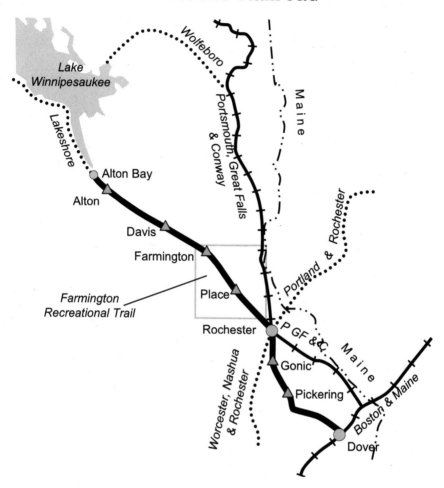

Dover to Alton Bay

Built: 1847–51

Abandoned: Farmington–Alton Bay, 1942; Dover–Gonic, 1943; Gonic–Rochester, 1983; Rochester–Farmington, 1995

"Cochecho" was the name of the river that the railroad right of way followed, and it was also the original name for Dover. Although "Cocheco" is the common spelling for the river now, the town and railroad used the additional "h" in the final syllable.

The Cochecho Railroad was built in the same late 1840s period as the Northern Railroad. Had it been able to connect to the Boston, Concord & Montreal, it would have been much more successful. However, the Lake Shore Railroad connection was not completed until 1890.

The Boston & Maine Railroad operated the Cochecho from 1864. The B&M concentrated on the Dover-to-Rochester section, which connected two important manufacturing towns, competing with the Eastern Railroad. North of Rochester, the line primarily served small farming communities.

The B&M attempted to use the Cochecho and Lake Shore Railroads, steamboats, and hotels to make a successful business out of summer vacationers visiting Lake Winnipesaukee. The shortness of the summer season made it difficult to support a railroad, and competition from automobiles dealt the final blow. Nearly all of the Lake Shore Railroad was abandoned in 1935, and the Farmington-to-Alton Bay segment of the Cochecho in 1942. Fortunately, some freight traffic preserved the Rochester-to-Farmington stretch until 1993, so the state of New Hampshire was able to buy it in 1995 for $200,000. It is now the Farmington Recreational Trail (see below).

The *New Hampshire State Trails Plan* described a portion of the Cochecho Railroad right of way as having been turned into the Lilac City Greenway in Rochester. However, two scouting trips to explore this greenway found nothing that looked like a rail trail or linear park—only some ordinary sidewalks.

The city of Dover plans to develop a Dover Community Trail using parts of the Cochecho Railroad right of way. This four-mile trail is past the planning stages and has federal and city funding.

CE1. Farmington Recreational Trail

Davidson Drive, Farmington, to Route 125, Rochester, 8.2 miles
Trail condition: ★ ★ ★ Rocky and sandy, but no major problems.
Scenery: ★ ★ ★ Mill ruins and a view of the Cocheco River, but near Route 11 most of the way.
Permitted uses: Non-motorized travel year-round; snowmobiles and OHRVs permitted in winter only when snow-covered.
Right of way owned by: State of New Hampshire for 6.8 miles. Trail ends may be privately owned, but they are marked with standard New Hampshire trail barriers.

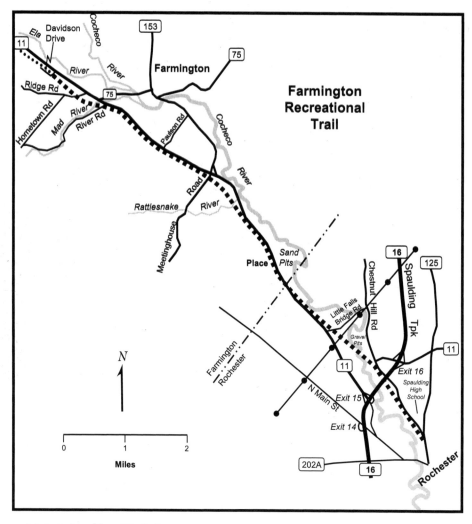

Maintained by: Trails Bureau.

ACCESS

The northern access is at Davidson Drive in Farmington, slightly north of Ridge Road. Davidson Drive is the driveway for the Collins & Aikman plant, but there is room to park a couple of cars by the trailhead. The southern terminus is Route 125 at the intersection of Chestnut Hill Road in Rochester. However, this is a busy street with no parking. If you want to start from the south, it would be better to start slightly north of there, perhaps at Spaulding High School.

The mill ruins at the Mad River crossing are the scenic highlight of this trail.

DESCRIPTION

The good news is that this section of the Cochecho Railroad right of way has been preserved as a trail. The bad news is that it does not have very interesting scenery, since it closely follows Route 11 for most of the way. Also, a rocky and sandy surface makes this trail a workout on a bicycle. It is most interesting to snowmobile and OHRV users in winter.

The trail starts with some separation from the highway. About a quarter of a mile beyond Ridge Road, you reach the highlight of this trail, the mill dam and sluiceway ruins at the Mad River crossing. Plan to spend some time looking around here.

From there, the trail goes by an uninspiring, seemingly endless stretch of Route 11, best described with a picture.

The trail crosses Route 11 at grade near the location of the Place station and the Farmington-Rochester border. After it crosses Little Falls Bridge Road in

The scenery along busy Route 11 is less than thrilling.

Rochester, the trail moves away from Route 11 toward Chestnut Hill Road. There is more to look at here. First you cross under a set of power lines, then over a calm stretch of the Cocheco River. An old gravel pit is marked by rusting machinery that looks like an artist's attempt at junk sculpture. The trail passes Spaulding High School before reaching the southern end at Route 125.

Cocheco River downstream from the railroad bridge

Wolfeboro Railroad

Wolfeboro to Sanbornville
Built: 1869–70
Abandoned: 1986

Wolfeboro is another town name like Peterborough or Hillsborough that can be spelled with or without an "ough" ending. I'm sticking with the railroad's shortened name, which is the official one on the town's web site.

This little railroad was a spur off of the Portsmouth, Great Falls & Conway Railroad that brought tourists to Lake Wentworth and Lake Winnipesaukee. Wolfeboro prides itself on being the "oldest summer resort in America." Governor John Wentworth started it all with a summer mansion built in the eighteenth century. It is a National Historic Site and one of Wolfeboro's tourist attractions.

The Eastern Railroad controlled both the PGF&C and Wolfeboro Railroads. It used them to compete with the Boston & Maine-controlled Cochecho and Lake Shore Railroad's access to the southern shores of Lake Winnipesaukee. The Wolfeboro Railroad also carried freight from local industries. These included wood products, woolen blankets, shoes, clay pipes, dairy products, pewter, and clothes.

The B&M Railroad operated the Wolfeboro Railroad between 1884 and 1972, by which time even on-demand freight traffic had dwindled to almost nil. The B&M sought to abandon the line, but instead it was taken over by a group who revived the Wolfeboro Railroad name and ran tourist trains until 1984. This venture petered out under competitive pressures from the Conway Scenic Railroad and the Hobo Railroad.

Wolfeboro's splendid depot has been beautifully preserved.

The state of New Hampshire then bought the line, with tracks in place. Antique section car enthusiasts use the tracks from Wolfeboro to Route 16. In addition, Wolfeboro created a four-season trail through that town by making a unique rail-with-trail configuration described under Trail CE2 (Bridge Falls Path and Cotton Valley Trail). Unfortunately, Brookfield has not done the same with its part of the right of way; but the trail is walkable from Route 16 in Wakefield to Turntable Park, Sanbornville (at the old junction with the Portsmouth, Great Falls & Conway Railroad).

CE2. Bridge Falls Path and Cotton Valley Trail (Wolfeboro Branch Recreational Trail)

[Note: The map shows the entire Wolfeboro Branch Recreational Trail, but the trail descriptions are by town, since local trail names and characteristics vary in each town.]

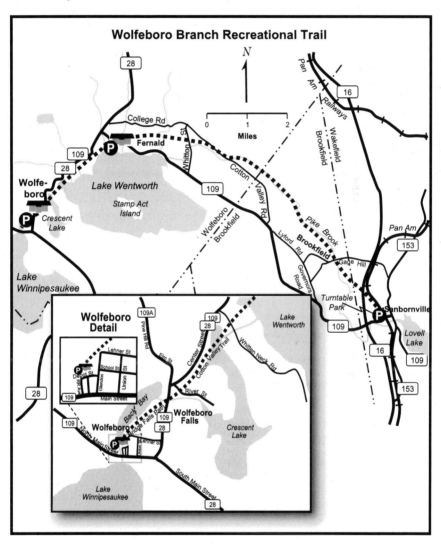

Lake Winnipesaukee to Cotton Valley Road, Wolfeboro, 6 miles

Trail condition: ★ ★ ★ ★ Good hardpack surface, but in-place track makes the trail narrow, and railroad ties under the hardpack will make for increasingly bumpy riding for bicyclists over time.

Scenery: ★ ★ ★ ★ ★ Excellent views of lakes and rivers.

Permitted uses: Railroad section cars (also called speeder cars or putt putts) and non-motorized travel year-round; snowmobiles and OHRVs permitted in winter only when snow-covered. Motorized trail bikes have caused damage to the rails by kicking up sand. They are definitely prohibited outside of winter.

Right of way owned by: State of New Hampshire.

Maintained by: Trails Bureau, Cotton Valley Rail Trail Club, and the Trails Rails Action Committee (TRAC) of Wolfeboro, Brookfield, and Wakefield.

ACCESS

To reach the western trailhead at the fanciful Wolfeboro Depot, take Route 109 west (North Main Street) from its junction with Route 28 in Wolfeboro (see Wolfeboro Detail map). Turn right on a short street called Railroad Avenue and look for the depot at (you guessed it) Depot Street. Parking is available at the depot. Parking can also be found at the old depot and maintenance build-

Bridge Falls Path follows the southeast shore of Back Bay.

In many sections, the narrow right of way required constructing the trail between the rails, such as here at Crescent Lake.

ing at Fernald, where Route 109 crosses the trail north of Lake Wentworth. The eastern end of this section of trail is the Cotton Valley Road crossing.

DESCRIPTION

This funky trail breaks all the rules but is both fun and scenic, so I heartily recommend it to anyone who gets close to the eastern end of Lake Winnipesaukee.

Bicycle trails are supposed to be at least ten feet wide. This one is four-and-a-half feet in many places. Rail trails should not cover up railroad ties, as that tends to make a lumpy surface. The Cotton Valley Trail has long stretches built between the existing rails, with hardpack covering the ties. This was done to accommodate collectors of old-time section cars, small track-riding vehicles that were originally used to check on track conditions. The narrow width makes bicyclists ride slowly, which is appropriate, since many walkers enjoy outings on the trail. Moreover, a slight bumpiness in the trail is not a big problem here.

Views vary from water scenes of Back Bay, Crescent Lake, and Lake Wentworth to woods and brooks. As you proceed eastward, the resort-town feeling of Wolfeboro gives way to increasingly remote scenes. The rich variety and attractiveness of cultural and natural objects along this trail deserve the five-star scenery rating.

The mile at the western end of this trail, called the Bridge Falls Path, has no track. Beyond Wolfeboro Falls, the track starts, and the locals call it the Cotton Valley Trail. Unless you are riding the rails, it is really all one trail from the Wolfeboro station to Cotton Valley Road.

Starting out from Wolfeboro, be sure to admire the ornate two-story Victorian depot with steeple, beautifully renovated by the town. Just beyond it, the freight house (privately owned) is also in excellent condition.

The Bridge Falls Path proceeds along a peaceful inlet of Lake Winnepesaukee now called Back Bay. Originally the railroad traveled between two bays, Front Bay to the northwest and Back Bay to the southeast. The town filled in Back Bay to create playing fields and then renamed the remaining body of water Back Bay, resulting in great confusion for map makers.

A small bridge crosses the stream from Crescent Lake to Back Bay at Wolfeboro Falls. Shortly thereafter, the path meets the start of track and changes name to Cotton Valley Trail. It immediately reaches the northern arm of another attractive body of water, Crescent Lake. A causeway over the tip of the lake gives more fine views.

Trail beside the rails northeast of Crescent Lake

NEW HAMPSHIRE RAIL TRAILS

Beaver pond view by the newly constructed trail

The trail alternates between sections located beside the track and those where the right of way was too narrow, so the trail was located between the rails. It seems strange, and I don't recommend this as a general approach, but it works on this trail.

After crossing Whitten Neck Road, you come to another causeway over the western edge of Lake Wentworth. Hills surround the lake, and it contains a forested island with the quaint name of Stamp Act Island. Colonial governor John Wentworth established a summer residence here in 1771, and Wolfeboro now uses the motto, "The Oldest Summer Resort in America."

A few hundred yards past the Lake Wentworth causeway, the trail diverges off of the railroad right of way for a short distance. You may want to take a short side trip to the New Hampshire Boat Museum (www.nhbm.org) to examine its vintage mahogany and antique boats. Back on the railroad right of way, lake views are behind you as the trail passes through a wooded region.

Fernald is a particularly interesting railroad stop. It had a small depot and a railroad maintenance facility. Both were restored and are maintained by the

Fernald depot and maintenance building have been nicely restored.

Cotton Valley Rail Trail Club as a storage and launching area for their section cars.

The two-and-a-half miles between Fernald and Cotton Valley Road were the object of a major trail construction project in 2006 and 2007. The project repaired bridges over brooks and replaced rotten ties before covering them with hardpack. As a result, this is now a pleasant stretch of trail. It traverses woodlands, with an open view by a beaver pond.

As of this writing, the trail ends at Cotton Valley Road. The next entry describes how it could continue through Brookfield in the future.

Proposed Brookfield Trail

Cotton Valley Road, Wolfeboro, to Route 16, Wakefield, 4.8 miles

(See Wolfeboro Branch Recreational Trail map, page 237.)

This five-mile section of railroad right is officially part of the state's Wolfeboro Branch Recreational Trail. However, as yet there has been no attempt to improve it for four-season use. Certainly riding a bicycle is out of the question, as one needs to bump along the railroad ties. Even trying to walk on the ties is not worth the effort. Hence, this stretch is only usable for section car outings in summer and for cross country skiing, snowmobiles, and OHRVs in winter. Most of this section is in Brookfield, and that town will have to be fully involved with efforts to construct a four-season, multi-use trail.

Two examples of section cars (also called speeder cars or putt putts) used on the Wolfeboro Branch Recreational Trail.

Because of the difficulty walking along this stretch, I only explored the two ends. It appears to have a remote feeling as it passes through the woods along Pike Brook, which connects Lovell Lake and Lake Wentworth.

Route 16 at the eastern end in Wakefield is a heavily traveled road and a major barrier. Section cars are not allowed east of the highway; in any case, the rails are buried under the pavement. On the other side of 16, Wakefield has established a short walkers-only trail (CE3; see below).

CE3. Wakefield Heritage Trail (Wolfboro Branch Recreational Trail)

(See map on page 237.)

Route 16 to Route 109, Wakefield, 0.7 mile

Trail condition: ★ ★ ★ Good path on the eastern end, but it deteriorates near Route 16. Track is still in place.

Scenery: ★ ★ ★ ★ Turntable Park, woods.

Permitted uses: Walking only.

Right of way owned by: State of New Hampshire and private owners.

Maintained by: Town of Wakefield.

Locomotive turntable. Note the active Pan Am Railways track to the right.

ACCESS

Access is at Turntable Park off Route 109 just west of the active Pan Am Railways track. There is plenty of parking at the park.

DESCRIPTION

Turntable Park is worth a visit to see the restored locomotive turntable. While there, you should take a stroll on this short greenway. West of the park, a trail next to the railroad track gradually peters out. Near Route 16 it is gone completely, and completing the journey to the highway requires walking on the ties of the track.

Eventually, when the Brookfield section is constructed as a multi-use trail, Turntable Park could be a great place to start or end an excursion. However, a sign at the park indicates that the trail is for walking only, so bicycles may not be allowed on this stretch.

Portsmouth, Great Falls & Conway Railroad

Jewett, ME, to Intervale
Built: 1848–72
Abandoned: Jewett–Somersworth, 1941; Mt. Whittier–Conway, 1972;
Ossipee Aggregates–Mt. Whittier, 1998

With woods, river crossings, mountains, and wetlands, the twenty-one-mile stretch between Ossipee and Conway has excellent scenery potential.

This railroad's location would seem to be an important north-south route in eastern New Hampshire, but it never carried much traffic or became very profitable. It was one of the fronts in the great battle between the Eastern and Boston & Maine Railroads. Now much of it is held by the state in hopes of encouraging railroad use, and parts of the line are still in operation.

Started under the names of the Great Falls & South Berwick and the Great Falls & Conway Railroads, this railroad gradually built track from Jewett, ME, to Union in 1855. Bankruptcies, reorganizations, and sparring between the Eastern and B&M finally led to the Eastern organizing the Portsmouth, Great Falls & Conway Railroad in 1865. Construction started again in 1870, and the railroad finally met the Portland & Ogdensburg Railroad at Intervale in 1875. The B&M took over control in 1885.

It appears that this line never became a major through route, other than to take vacationers up to North Conway and the White Mountains. It eked out a marginal existence serving manufacturers of lumber, woolen cloth, quarry granite, and furniture.

Guilford, the B&M's successor, gave up on the line, which it sold to the state of New Hampshire. Freight trains operated by New Hampshire Northcoast Corporation run up to Ossipee Aggregates, and Conway Scenic Railroad trains use the track from Conway north. In between, there are twenty-one miles of scenic railroad right of way with the same unused status as the Wilton line up to Bennington in the Southwest Region. No trains run through there, but the state is holding onto the track. The *New Hampshire State Trails Plan* describes this section as having potential as a trail but says there are no plans for trail development due to "high potential for return of rail service." One wonders if that is true, given impediments such as the grade-level crossing of busy Route 16.

The Bureau of Trails web site refers to these twenty-one miles as the Conway Branch Recreational Trail and says that permitted uses are non-motorized travel plus snowmobiles, ATVs, and trail bikes when snow-covered. In reality, use is restricted to winter activities except for short stretches with informal

There is an informal path beside the track for a short distance.

The impressive Bearcamp River truss bridge near Lake Ossipee is fully decked for snowmobile use, while keeping the rails usable.

paths beside the track. Walking on the railroad ties for any distance is an unpleasant experience.

I explored about five miles of this right of way near Center Ossipee (where the Mountain View station was located) in June 2007. Although a passable informal trail exists beside the track for a few miles on both sides of Center Ossipee, it is dangerously close to the drop-off at the side of fills, prone to erosion, and peters out so that further travel requires walking the ties.

Ossipee planners are aware of the excellent potential this section has for a four-season trail. If you would like to help with the effort to make this trail a reality, contact the Ossipee Planning Board or Conservation Commission.

North Region

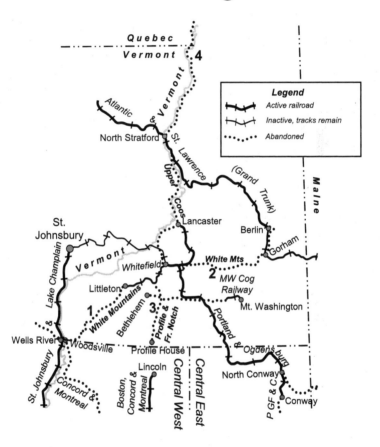

Legend
Active railroad
Inactive, tracks remain
Abandoned

T HE North Region extends from Vermont in the west to the Maine border in the east and from the Canadian border south to Woodsville and Conway. This remote mountainous region once saw extensive activity from three major railroads, but today there is almost no railroad traffic. What

Attracted by scenery like this view of Mounts Madison and Adams from Route 2 in Randolph, tourists have flocked to this region since the mid-nineteenth century.

does remain is tourist traffic on the Conway Scenic Railroad and the venerable Mount Washington Cog Railway. Some freight hauls occur on a sporadic, as needed basis on the "active" lines, but you will be lucky ever to see a train.

The major lines originated as the White Mountains, the Portland & Ogdensburg, and the Atlantic & St. Lawrence Railroads. The White Mountains line (quickly absorbed by the Boston, Concord & Montreal) served numerous tourist locations north of the Presidential Range, as well as forest products freight. It provided the right of way for the two major rail trails in the North Region, the Ammonoosuc Recreational Trail (N1) and the Presidential Range Trail (N2). The Portland & Ogdensburg offered both tourist service to the high mountains and through traffic from Boston and Portland to Canada. The Atlantic & St. Lawrence was built to provide service between Portland and Montreal. It was soon acquired by the Grand Trunk Railroad, a precursor to the Canadian National Railways. The Grand Trunk connected the eastern British territories in North America. The need for cooperation among the various territories to build the railroad helped push the federation that later became Canada.

The Upper Coos Railroad was a minor line that served wood products industries. It lives on in rail trails because the state of New Hampshire bought two sections in the 1970s. One of these is important for the Pondicherry section of the Presidential Range Rail Trail; the other is located in the far northern towns of Colebrook and Stewartstown.

Two other railroads, the famous Mount Washington Cog Railway and the Profile & Franconia Notch Railroad, were built for the tourist trade. The Cog Railway was constructed immediately after the Civil War. Several railroads in Europe imitated its ingenuous construction, which allowed steep climbs in mountainous areas. Amazingly, this rickety-looking railroad, built on miles of steep trestles going up Mount Washington, still carries passengers to see the views almost 140 years after its construction. The Profile & Franconia Notch served the magnificent Profile House hotel. After the railroad was abandoned, Route 3 took most of its right of way. However, there is a short but special rail trail north of Route 3.

The major lines provided jumping off points for a number of logging railroads that sprang up in the late nineteenth and early twentieth centuries. J. E.

J. E. Henry's East Branch & Lincoln Railroad served the most notorious of the clear-cutting operations. This locomotive and log truck are on display at Loon Mountain.

Henry's line along the East Branch of the Pemigewasset River was the most notorious. Timber railroads, hastily constructed and designed for short lifetimes, moved masses of logs from clear-cut forest areas to nearby mills. Major railroads then carried the sawed lumber to urban markets. The logging railroads served their purpose so well that the northern New Hampshire forests were completely stripped. Often the slash from the clear cutting would catch fire from locomotive sparks, resulting in massive forest fires. Public outcry over this destruction of the beautiful mountain scenery resulted in passage of the Weeks Act in 1911, which called for acquisition of land for the White Mountains National Forest. Since then, nature has taken over, and the forest has regenerated. Once again, the region is beautiful to behold and well worth visiting.

Most of the logging railroad corridors have been taken up by roads. Some have been partly incorporated into Forest Service trails. The only trail that I know of that goes a long distance on a logging railroad is the Wilderness Trail. It starts at a Forest Service parking lot where the Kancamagus Highway goes away from the East Branch of the Pemigewasset River. J. E. Henry's clear cutting in this area is now the Pemigewasset Wilderness.

White Mountains Railroad (Boston, Concord & Montreal)

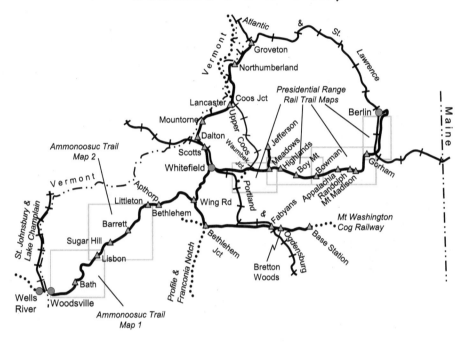

Wells River, VT, to Groveton
Branches: Mt. Washington: Wing Road–Cog Railway Base Station; **White-field & Jefferson:** Whitefield–Berlin; **Waumbec:** Meadows–Jefferson
Built: 1848–95
Abandoned: Waumbec Branch, 1925; Mt. Washington Branch, 1938; Whitefield–Lancaster, 1941; Lancaster–Coos Jct., 1980; Waumbek Jct.–Berlin, 1996; Woodsville–Littleton, 1996.

The White Mountains Railroad passed through several owners and grew slowly to its fullest extent, as shown on the map. It then slowly declined, leaving only the Littleton-to-Whitefield section in operational condition.

The original White Mountains charter was for a line from Wells River, VT, to Groveton, thereby connecting the Atlantic & St. Lawrence Railroad with the Boston, Concord & Montreal branch proposed from Plymouth to Woodsville. Initial service, run by the BC&M, started in 1853 but only covered the distance between Wells River and Littleton. Extension to Lancaster was delayed until 1870, after the BC&M acquired the White Mountains. The White Mountains

The three-story Woodsville Depot

Line of the BC&M progressed to Groteton in 1872 to finally meet with the Atlantic & St. Lawrence's successor, the Grand Trunk. The BC&M's successor after merger with the Concord RR, the Concord & Montreal, completed the various branches, including the long bridge over the GT and the Androscog-

Although condemned for railroad use, the Connecticut River bridge could be decked for a trail connection between Woodsville and Wells River.

The ball signal in Whitefield at the junction of the Portland & Ogdensburg and White Mountains Railroads. The train with the raised ball had the right of way. Once common, this is the last ball signal in New England.

gin River to reach Berlin. Traffic was a combination of tourists and lumber freight from large wood and paper operations.

The Boston & Maine took over in 1895. In the twentieth-century period of decline in railroading, the B&M gradually abandoned the branches. After Guilford acquired the B&M, they decided not to run trains east of Woodsville, and they leased the track to the New Hampshire & Vermont Railroad. Condemnation of the bridge over the Connecticut River discouraged the NH&VT operation.

Both the Wells River-to-Littleton and Waumbek Junction-to-Berlin sections were abandoned recently, so the state of New Hampshire was able to buy them and preserve them to become two of the state's finest rail trails.

The only stretches that are marginally operational today are Littleton-to-Whitefield, owned by Pan Am Railways, and Whitefield to Waumbek Junction, owned by the state and operated by the New Hampshire Central Railroad. Trains are very rare here, and they can only go five miles per hour on the deteriorated track.

N1. Ammonoosuc Recreational Trail

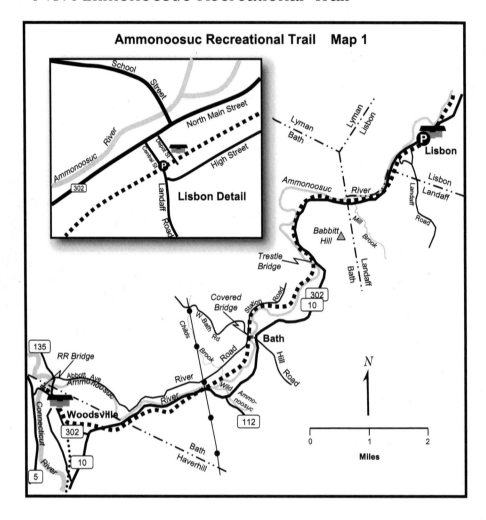

Central Street (Route 302), Woodsville, to Industrial Park Drive, Littleton, 19 miles

Trail condition: ★★★ Easily rideable and walkable most of the way, but the surface is rough. Some short sections are particularly tough going due to ballast rock.

Scenery: Woodsville–Lisbon, ★★★★★ Excellent views of the free-flowing Ammonoosuc River away from roads, and covered bridge and falls in Bath; **Lisbon–Littleton,** ★★★ More views of the Ammonoosuc River and

The long bridge over the Ammonoosuc River presents expansive views of the river.

a nice overlook of the Gale River, but this section is more built-up and the trail is close to roads the whole way.

Permitted uses: Non-motorized travel plus ATVs, motorized trail bikes, and snowmobiles.

Right of way owned by: State of New Hampshire.

Maintained by: Trails Bureau and Littleton Offroad Riders.

ACCESS

For the Woodsville-to-Lisbon stretch, you have several choices of access points at both ends, and it may be possible to park and pick up the trail at the covered bridge in Bath. Otherwise, it is a remote trail without road access. In Woodsville, the trail starts in the center of town next to Central Street at the Elm Street intersection (see Woodsville Trailhead map, Trail CW6, page 225), but you can start anywhere along Central Street up to the Job Lot store. Although there is no formal trail parking, you should be able to park at the Job Lot store or on one of the side streets off Central. At the Lisbon end, the trail is one block south of Main Street (Route 302). There is a parking area for the trail where it crosses Lisbon's Central Street (Landaff Road), as shown on the Lisbon Detail map.

For the Lisbon-to-Littleton stretch, there is nearly continuous access along River Road and Mount Eustis Road. Both Route 117 and River Road have bridges over the Ammonoosuc River, so it is easy to cross from the Routes 10/302 highway to the trail side. At the Littleton end, there is informal parking where the active Pan Am Railways track starts. Take combined Routes 10/302 to a stop light at a small shopping center at Industrial Park Road. Go south on Industrial Park, cross the river, and park on the left side, opposite the trail-head.

DESCRIPTION

The Ammonoosuc Recreational Trail is another long rail trail that divides neatly in half to make two more reasonable length outings. The 9.7-mile Woodsville-to-Lisbon stretch is a gem of a trail that gives you a close encounter with the free-flowing Ammonoosuc River as you traverse wooded areas remote from roads. The 9.1-mile Lisbon-to-Littleton stretch is quite different, as you travel by roads, houses, and fields the whole way. Both stretches allow ATVs and motorized trail bikes year-round, so you are likely to encounter them.

Woodsville-to-Lisbon

From the western start near Elm Street in Woodsville, the trail stays in town for a while. It veers away from Central Street where the Concord & Montreal Railroad junction was (above the Ocean State Job Lot store). After passing under a quaint wooden bridge and over Routes 10/302, the trail feels remote from civilization.

The bridge over the highway is covered with ballast rock, an uncomfortable surface to walk or ride on. In your next encounter with the highway, about two miles further, you duck under a high overpass. The trail then leads to one of the prime viewing spots, the long bridge that crosses the Ammonoosuc River at an angle. You can see a long distance both upstream and downstream along this beautiful river. A major tributary, the Wild Ammonoosuc River, merges with the main river on the south side. The trail soon crosses a small tributary, Childs Brook. Check out the elaborate granite foundation for this short, high bridge.

You'll want to get your camera out in Bath, where the trail passes under an exceptionally long covered bridge by some falls in the river. A sign on the west

The covered bridge and falls at Bath are a trail highlight.

entrance to the bridge indicates it was built in 1832 and says "One dollar fine to drive any team faster than a walk on this bridge." A Boston & Maine caboose sits where the depot used to be, north of the bridge.

Picturesque views of the meandering river and rolling hills follow for the next two miles until the trail comes to a second bridge across the river. This steel truss structure marks a major change in the feel of the trail, as it now follows the Routes 302/10 highway closely for the four miles to Lisbon. You are out of the woods and have more open views. The meandering Ammonoosuc River continues to be the scenery focus. Mill Brook enters the main river from the south in picturesque cascades. There are more views of the meandering river as well as the cascading Mill Brook when you cross it.

The third highway crossing is through a culvert in the middle of a short stretch of trail in the town of Landaff. The culvert crossing marks the approach into Lisbon.

Ballast problem on the Ammonoosuc Recreational Trail

While still operating trains, the Boston & Maine Railroad upgraded the entire right of way from Woodsville to Lisbon with heavy ballast rock. This provided a stable, well-drained foundation for the railroad ties. However, once the rails and ties were removed, the ballast made use of the trail hard for any purpose other than snowmobiles and cross country skiing when snow-covered. As on the Northern Rail Trail in Merrimack County, a significant program of ballast removal has made the trail ridable in the summer. However, in this case no hardpack was applied, so the entire trail from Woodsville is a little bumpy.

For some reason, ballast rock remains at all of the Trails Bureau gates. Grooves in the ballast made by trail bikes in the narrow openings by the gates can be a bit treacherous on bicycles, so riders may want to dismount and walk through.

After the ties were removed, the ballast rock made a very rough trail surface. (Dick Mackay)

This steel truss structure is the second bridge over the Ammonoosuc River.

Lisbon-to-Littleton

Before you leave Lisbon, be sure to admire the Lisbon depot. It has been re-stored using federal and state grants and extensive volunteer help. From there the trail crosses the highway at grade level and then affords views of the river. On my 2006 scout, there was a long stretch of ballast here, but it may have been improved by the time you read this.

An old house, barn, and nearby graveyard come before the next Routes 10/302 crossing under a high bridge. A small stream, Salmon Hole Brook, makes its dash toward the Ammonoosuc from the east.

The Lisbon Depot under renovation in 2006 as part of town revitalization managed by the Lisbon Main Street organization. The renovation was faithful to the original two-story design with sloped roof and quaint dormers.

For almost six miles, the trail stays very close to roads, first running beside two disconnected sections of River Road and then along Mount Eustis Road. The road surface is smoother than the trail, so bicyclists are tempted to ride on

The trail (right) is very close to River Road (left). Traffic is light on the road, and the road surface is more comfortable than the trail's for bicyclists.

the road to avoid vibration on the trail. Open views to the northwest show you both the river and Routes 10/302, plus factories and houses along the highway.

Half way through these six miles, the trail crosses the Gale River, a major tributary. The railroad bridge gives a great view of this stream as it descends to its confluence with the Ammonoosuc. The Gale River separates the two halves of River Road; the northern section begins with a bridge across the trail and the Ammonoosuc to Routes 10/302. Past this point, the trail continues wedged between the Ammonoosuc River and River Road/Mount Eustis Road until a half mile or so after you cross into Littleton. Then the road diverges from the river, while the trail stays close by it.

A double set of overpasses signals that you are passing under I-93. From there it is a short distance to the trail end at Industrial Park Road. You'll see railroad tracks and likely even a few freight cars on the other side of the in-

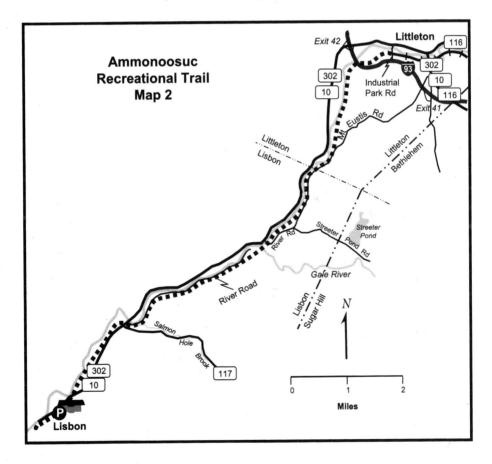

Gale River viewed from the rail trail

dustrial park driveway. This is the line that Pan Am Railways continues to own and use for occasional operations.

N2. Presidential Range Rail Trail

Airport Road, Whitefield, to Water Treatment Plant, Berlin, 23 miles
Trail condition: ★★★ Basically a good cinders surface, but rough riding for bicyclists; some issues with water on the trail and ballast rock.
Scenery: Pondicherry section: ★★★★★ Gorgeous views of mountains, Cherry Pond, wetlands, and wildlife; **Israel River section:** ★★★★ Israel River, Presidential Range, close to Valley Road; **Moose River section:** ★★★★★ Follows the Moose River through an isolated gorge; **Androscoggin section:** ★★★ Impressive Androscoggin River bridge and historical interest from Brown Company remains, but somewhat monotonous scenery north of the bridge.
Permitted uses: Non-motorized travel all year; snowmobiles, ATVs, and motorized trail bikes permitted in winter only when snow-covered.

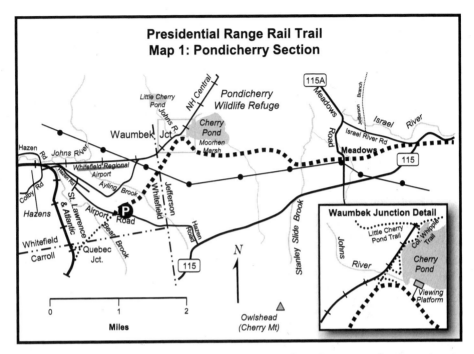

Presidential Range Rail Trail
Map 1: Pondicherry Section

Right of way owned by: State of New Hampshire for 20.2 miles from Airport Road to Gorham; ownership unknown for 3 miles up to Berlin. It is unclear where the state-owned right of way ends.

Maintained by: Trails Bureau, Friends of Pondicherry, Whitefield Sno-Kings, and Presidential Range Riders.

ACCESS

For the Airport Road access from Whitefield, take Hazen Road from Route 16 east of Whitefield. Cross the Johns River and the railroad tracks at Hazens, then jog right and left onto Airport Road (a renaming of the center section of Hazen Road). Proceed about a half mile beyond the Whitefield Regional Airport and turn left into the trailhead parking.

For the Airport Road access from the south, take Route 3 north to Route 115 north. Go about two-and-a-half miles and turn left onto Hazen Road after seeing an airport sign. This turns into Airport Road. Go about a mile and turn right into the trail parking area.

On the east end of the Pondicherry section, the Route 115A access at Meadows is easy to miss. I drove by it twice before finally locating it. Coming from the south, turn north from Route 115 onto 115A. Go down a hill and cross under the power lines. The trail is just beyond the power lines and before you come to a bridge over a brook. Coming from the north, take Meadows Road south from Jefferson to Route 115A. Continue past Israel River Road, go across the bridge over a brook, and stop before the power lines cross the road. There is very limited parking here.

The Bowman access at the east end of the Israel River section is off Route 2 in Randolph at a parking area with signs for hikers climbing the Castle Trail. There is a similar parking area for hikers off Route 2 at Appalachia, on the Moose River section, as well as access where the Dolly Copp-Pinkham Road crosses the trail.

A large parking lot for snowmobilers off Route 2 in Gorham (near Jimtown Road) gives access to the eastern end of the Moose River section and south-western end of the Androscoggin River section. The northern end of the Androscoggin section is the Berlin Water Treatment Plant. Take Mason Street east from Route 16, cross the river, then turn right on Devent Street and follow it south to the plant. Alternatively, you can begin or end your excursion at the Eastern Depot restaurant. From Mason Street, turn left onto Unity Street and park by the Eastern Depot, located at the corner of Mason and Unity.

DESCRIPTION

The Presidential Range Rail Trail is over 20 miles long, so I have divided it into four sections based on the ponds and rivers they follow:

- Pondicherry Section (3.7 miles)
- Israel River Section (6.4 miles)
- Moose River Section (8.6 miles)
- Androscoggin River Section (4.7 miles)

Weather makes a huge difference in your enjoyment of the Presidential Range Rail Trail. My first scout in October 2006 was on a cold, heavily overcast day. I could only see the lower 1500 feet of the surrounding mountains, and they didn't seem that impressive. Going back on a gorgeous day in June 2007, I finally understood why people rave about this trail.

This far north, the weather can be less predictable and forgiving than on the trails to the south. For example, I had snow on the trail in late October. Be prepared and dress appropriately.

On all sections of the Presidential Range Rail Trail, vibration from riding a rough surface may make bicyclists want to cover only a section or two of the trail per ride, rather than the whole trail at once. I felt the ride in my wrists and seat.

The place names—Meadows, Highlands, Boy Mountain, Bowman, Appalachia, Randolph, and Mount Madison—were all stops on the railroad. Unfortunately, the only remaining railroad artifact is the Highlands depot on the Israel River section.

Pondicherry Section
Airport Road, Whitefield, to Route 115A (Meadows), Jefferson, 3.7 miles

Almost all of the Pondicherry section is in the Pondicherry National Wildlife Refuge. It is part of the Silvio O. Conte National Fish and Wildlife Refuge, which protects a number of key wildlife habitats in the Connecticut River basin. Besides giving access to Cherry Pond and surrounding wetlands, this section of trail offers outstanding views of the Presidential Range and other mountains in the area.

David and Kathy Govatski ride toward Mount Waumbek. David heads the Friends of Pondicherry and is a leading proponent of the Presidential Range Rail Trail.

Because of the wetlands, black flies, mosquitos, and deer flies can be a problem. Try to pick a day with a breeze or wear protective clothing and bug repellent.

Here's what you see going east from Airport Road:

The trail starts in a northeast direction along the Upper Coos Railroad right of way, now a woodsy path with a cinders surface. Mount Waumbek shows up nicely in the clearing created by the path.

Waumbek Junction was where the Upper Coos and White Mountains Railroads crossed. As you reach the junction, the trail splits. The path to the right is the main trail, following the route of the White Mountains Railroad. I recommend you first go straight and explore the trails around the Waumbek Junction area. The junction had a depot and freight house, but the only remaining signs are the tracks from the two historic railroads and a siding.

A path along the Upper Coos track gives you views of Cherry Pond and access to the Colonel Whipple Trail to the northeast and the Little Cherry Pond Trail to the northwest. Be careful to cross the track at designated points only. The New Hampshire Central Railroad has restored service on this stretch between Whitefield and Lancaster, so it is an active rail line. Moreover, NHC will be using a siding near the junction for switching, so a train that has passed may return suddenly.

Cherry Pond view of the Presidential Range: Madison, Adams, Jefferson, and Washington

The trail tends to be wet going through Moorhen Marsh, south of Cherry Pond.

Back on the main Presidential Range Rail Trail, you come to a viewing platform that offers an outstanding view of the pond and surrounding mountains.

Continuing toward Meadows, you pass through a wet area caused by beavers clogging the culverts between Moorhen Marsh and Cherry Pond. Bicycles have no problem, as the water tends to be no more than an inch deep. If you are walking, make sure you have waterproof boots. Counteracting the water rise from beavers is a major concern for this trail.

Past Moorhen Marsh, the trail goes over a couple of short stretches of ballast rock and crosses Stanley Slide Brook. Then it reaches Route 115A at Meadows.

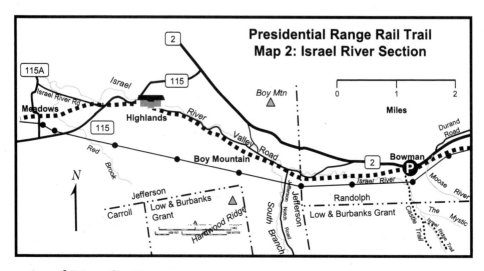

Israel River Section

Route 115A (Meadows), Jefferson, to Castle Trailhead (Bowman), Randolph, 6.4 miles

This section of the Presidential Range Rail Trail goes along the Israel River up to the pass at Bowman that made this route feasible for the railroad. It is more open than the other trail sections, and Valley Road is close by for a few miles. Still, the mountain views are excellent.

The Highlands depot is now a private residence. The snowmobile suggests that the owners enjoy living by the trail.

Winter scene? No, this snow on the trail was in October! The trail follows the river and gives views of the mountains.

Starting out from Route 115A, the trail goes east through second growth forest. Very soon it crosses Red Brook as that stream cascades down to meet the Israel River. About a mile further on, you cross a new section of Route 115. It was built a few years ago to straighten the road, and many maps still show the highway on the route now called Israel River Road. There is little parking at Route 115, and it is easy to drive past the trail without seeing it from that road.

In another half mile you pass by the Highlands depot, now maintained as a private residence. For the next few miles, the trail follows both the Israel River and Valley Road to the Jefferson-Randolph border. Trees along the trail hide Valley Road, and there are occasional views of the mountains.

At the South Branch, the railroad bridge provides a nice view of the rapids in this large tributary of the Israel. The trail then crosses Jefferson Notch Road, which rises steeply along the South Branch. Many hikers drive this road to a high elevation before starting on one of the many hiking trails. The road was constructed on the right of way of the South Branch Railroad, a Boston & Maine spur line that hauled logs for the Berlin Mills Company.

After leaving Valley Road, the trail continues along the gently meandering Israel River up to the Castle Trailhead parking area. This is a particularly scenic part of the trail with views of both the river and the high surrounding peaks. Trees keep the nearby power lines from being a major visual distraction.

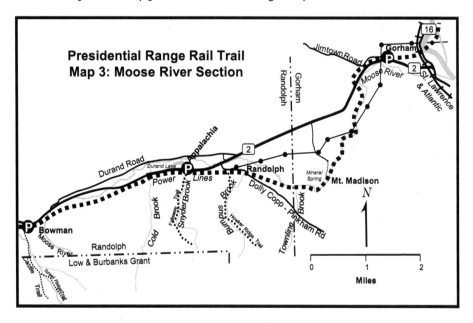

Moose River Section

Castle Trailhead (Bowman), Randolph, to Route 2 parking area, Gorham, 8.6 miles.

The Castle Trailhead parking area sits at the divide between the Israel and Moose Rivers. On this section, you descend along the rapidly falling Moose River on your way to Gorham. The remote feeling in this deep gorge and closeness to the rapids of the river give this section a high scenery rating. The sides of the trail are heavily wooded, so the power lines close by to the south are hardly ever visible.

Numerous hiking trails cross the rail trail. You'll see them at Bowman, Appalachia, and Randolph. One imagines scores of Appalachian Mountain Club hikers getting off trains at these stops ninety years ago and hiking up the Presidentials. Presumably the Appalachia stop was named for the club. When done, they would go to one of the stops and take a train back to Boston. Today the Appalachian Mountain Club runs buses shuttling hikers in much the same way, but now to their cars parked in the area.

Heading east from Bowman, the trail is a pleasant stroll through the woods for over two miles. The first major landmark is the crossing of Cold Brook, a dashing mountain stream. A half mile beyond, at Appalachia, you reach a large parking lot off Route 2. Hikers park here to climb along a large network of trails up to Mount Adams and Mount Madison. The Appalachian Mountain Club's *White Mountain Guide* contains excellent maps of these trails.

Take a close look at the unusual bridge crossing Snyder Brook, near Appalachia. It is a wooden pony truss bridge, meaning that the triangular truss structure is above the bridge deck, and there is no triangular truss structure under the deck. The wooden trusses are boxed and have slanted roofs to shed rain and snow. This is the only example of this type of bridge that I've seen in New Hampshire. Apparently the concept is sound, as this wooden bridge still stands after the better part of a century.

About one-and-a-third miles after Snyder Brook, the trail crosses Dolly Copp-Pinkham Road, the site of the railroad's Randolph stop. This is the only road crossing for the Moose River stretch of the Presidential Range Rail Trail until you come to the Gorham end. Just beyond the road, you cross a stream with the fanciful name Bumpus Brook.

Unusual boxed pony truss bridge over Snyder Brook

One of many Moose River crossings

Two miles after Dolly Copp-Pinkham Road, the river and trail enter the gorge that is the scenic highlight of this section. The trail crosses the Moose River many times on sturdy steel bridges well decked for snowmobiles.

When the gorge changes direction and heads northeast, you come to the site of the Mount Madison station. This stop was apparently used to take passengers to a nearby mineral spring. The area is now accessible by either the rail trail or a trail that descends the gorge from a dirt road on the north side. Unfortunately I did not realize I should be looking for the spring on my scout and hence did not notice any artifacts.

Two miles further on, the trail departs from the river and goes under a high bridge for Route 2. Near Jimtown Road, the highway has descended to the same level as the rail trail, and there is a huge parking area.

Androscoggin River Section
Route 2 parking area, Gorham, to Water Treatment Plant, Berlin, 4.7 miles

The scenery here is not as gorgeous as on other stretches of the Presidential Range Rail Trail. However, it provides a look at interesting aspects of the Brown Paper Company operations and includes the long, impressive Androscoggin bridge.

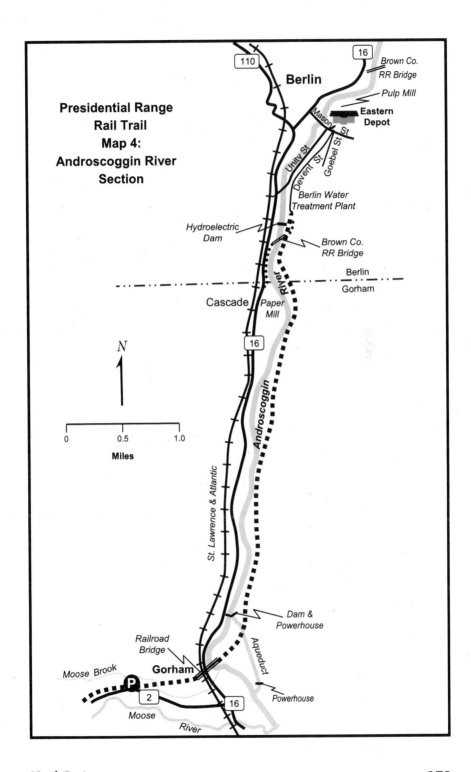

Presidential Range
Rail Trail
Map 4:
Androscoggin River
Section

Berlin

110

16

Brown Co.
RR Bridge

Pulp Mill

Eastern
Depot

Mason St

Goebel St

Devent St

Unity St

Berlin Water
Treatment Plant

Hydroelectric
Dam

Brown Co.
RR Bridge

Berlin
Gorham

Cascade

River

Paper
Mill

16

N

0   0.5   1.0

Miles

Androscoggin

St. Lawrence & Atlantic

Dam &
Powerhouse

Aqueduct

Railroad
Bridge

Moose Brook

Gorham

P

2

16

Powerhouse

Moose

River

The railroad bridge gives you a spectacular crossing of the Androscoggin River.

Traveling east from the Route 2 parking area, the trail crosses Moose Brook, a tributary of the Moose River, on a new snowmobile bridge. Sitting behind the new bridge are the charred remains of the old railroad bridge, a monument to the wooden bridge arson that plagues New Hampshire.

The main attraction of this trail section is the long bridge over the Androscoggin River, about half a mile east of Moose Brook. It crosses the river, Route 16, and the St. Lawrence & Atlantic Railroad tracks on the west side of the river, and it provides excellent views of the river, both upstream and downstream.

Soon after crossing the railroad and river, you come to another bridge across an aqueduct that carries water between two power plants. On the east side of the river, the trail settles into a steady pattern in Gorham. There are some views of free-flowing river, plus outlooks onto power plants; but most of the way has little view and all looks the same. Utility lines follow alongside the trail. Bikers will have to walk on some long ballast rock sections.

Just south of the Berlin line, you see the big Cascade paper mill complex on the other side of the river. Just beyond that view, the trail goes through a small rock cut. When the view opens up again, there is a strange sight: a small bridge crossing the river at an angle. It looks like a railroad bridge, but has three large pipes on it. My first guess was that it was connected to the Berlin Water Treatment Plant, but it actually was a Brown Company railroad bridge turned into a platform for pipes carrying a pulp slurry and clean water to the Cascade mill to make paper.

I rode the trail twice and wasn't able to tell where the state-owned portion ends. However, north of the Great Lakes Hydro dam (just upstream from the Brown Company railroad bridge) the B&M right of way deteriorates as a trail. It is covered with large ballast rock and not worth trying to walk or ride. Fortunately, Devent Street is close by and makes a convenient, low-traffic route. Detour onto Devent Street when you see the Berlin water treatment plant.

I recommend continuing north on Devent to Mason Street. There you will see the old Eastern Depot located on the corner of Mason and Unity Streets. It was called the Eastern Depot because the Grand Trunk Line had a depot in Berlin on the west side of the river. Beyond the depot is the Berlin pulp mill complex, slated for demolition as part of a Berlin urban renewal project.

This is the best view of the free-flowing Androscoggin River.

THE BROWN COMPANY

Berlin grew up as a forest products mill town, using the abundant supply of timber in the Great North Woods and water power from the Androscoggin falls at Berlin and Cascade. The first Berlin sawmill was built in 1852 by H. Winslow & Co. A short company railroad built in 1865 crossed the river to meet the Atlantic & St. Lawrence Railroad. William Wentworth Brown bought controlling interest in H. Winslow & Co. and changed the name to Berlin Mills in 1866. Brown and his sons (not related to the Browns of Brown's Lumber Co. in Whitefield) pioneered the sulphite process for paper making and built the huge Cascade mill to produce pulp and newsprint in 1903. At the time, it was the largest, most modern paper mill in the world. A company railroad brought logs across the river to this vertically integrated complex that went from de-barking logs to producing finished paper. In 1917 the Berlin Mills Company changed name to the Brown Company. Later, the company moved its pulp operations to Berlin and sent the pulp as a slurry through a pipe across the little railroad bridge. Other pipes carried clean water, as the Androscoggin River water was too polluted for the plant to use.

The company went under during the Depression, was reorganized, and eventually (1966) became part of Gulf & Western Industries, who sold it in 1980 to James River. The old plants gradually lost economic viability. The pulp mill in Berlin was closed in 2006, and the paper mill at Cascade was threatened with closure at the end of 2007.

Cascade mill complex

Profile & Franconia Notch Railroad

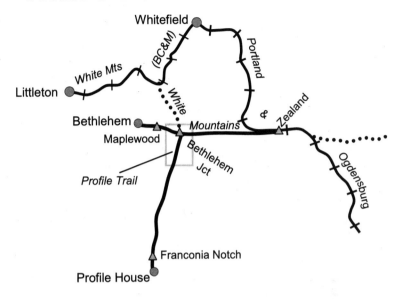

Zealand to Profile House
Bethlehem & Maplewood Division: Bethlehem–Bethlehem Jct.
Built: 1879–81
Abandoned: Bethlehem Jct.–Profile House, 1921; Bethlehem–Bethlehem Jct., 1925; Bethlehem Jct.–Zealand, 1938

Charles Greenleaf and Richard Taft built the narrow-gauge Profile & Franconia Notch Railroad to provide a convenient way for vacationers to get to their Profile House hotel. A spectacular resort in the heart of Franconia Notch, Profile House had been losing customers to other resort hotels that did not require a rough three-hour carriage ride from Littleton.

In 1881 the railroad added a branch to Maplewood and Bethlehem, primarily to serve the Maplewood resort hotel. It joined the Profile & Franconia Notch branch at Bethlehem Junction on the west side of the Ammonoosuc River.

This line was taken over by the Concord & Montreal Railroad in 1893 and then by the Boston & Maine Railroad when it won the New Hampshire railroad wars. The B&M replaced the narrow-gauge track with standard gauge in 1896. The line to Profile House was abandoned in 1921. Later, construction of the Route 3 highway to Franconia Notch took over much of the right of way.

*Narrow-gauge train at the Profile House Depot. The depot
was tucked away in the woods to avoid spoiling the beautiful
views from Profile House. (Courtesy of Milne Special
Collections, University of New Hampshire Library)*

A short section south of Bethlehem Junction remains, however, and is now a
rail trail.

N3. Profile Recreational Trail

Muchmore Road to Route 3, Bethlehem, 2 miles

Trail condition: ★ ★ ★ A beautiful but fragile grassy surface, sometimes blocked by fallen balsam fir trees.

Scenery: ★ ★ ★ ★ ★ The grassy trail surface, views of hills, and wetlands in a remote-feeling setting make a surprisingly attractive trail.

Permitted uses: Non-motorized travel year-round; snowmobiles, ATVs, and motorized trail bikes in winter only when snow-covered. Bicyclists should be careful not to ride on the fragile surface when it is muddy.

Right of way owned by: State of New Hampshire. A short distance on the north end may be privately owned.

Maintained by: U.S. Forest Service.

The trail heading toward Scarface and Bickford Mountains

ACCESS

There are four easy access points: the northern trailhead on Muchmore Road near the intersection of Route 302; the Trudeau Road crossing about two-

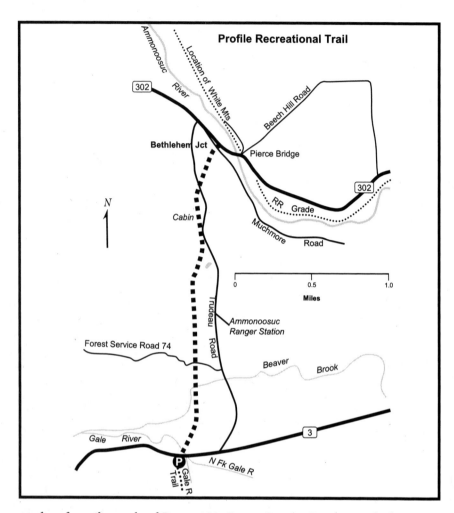

Profile Recreational Trail

tenths of a mile south of Route 302; Forest Service Road 74, which crosses about six-tenths of a mile north of Route 3; and on Route 3, opposite the Gale River trailhead. The only convenient place to park multiple cars is at the Gale River Trail parking area.

DESCRIPTION

I expect few people to make a long drive to go on such a short trail. But if you are in the area, this trail is worth experiencing. The soft grassy surface, lack of

The trail was clear in October 2006, but many trees had fallen when I scouted again in June 2007.

traffic, views of wetlands and hills, and a sense of discovery made me fall in love with it. I never saw anyone else on the trail on either of my two scouts, or even evidence that other people were using it. Walking may be more appropriate than bicycling given the grassy surface and short distance.

This is marked as part of the Heritage Trail. Presumably a new trail under development by the Forest Service will link it with the paved bicycle path through Franconia Notch.

Going south from the quaintly named Muchmore Road, the trail passes through birch forest. After the Trudeau Road crossing, the trees are mostly balsam fir. These short-lived trees have a tendency to fall over. On my June 2007 scout there were fifteen to twenty of them across the trail, but they were easy to step over. A Forest Service ranger said they would clean up the trail, but a cutback in maintenance funds had created a backlog of such work.

Just south of Trudeau Road, you come to a small cabin, apparently owned by the Forest Service. From there the trail proceeds on a carpet of greenery through woods and wetlands, with a few views of surrounding mountains.

Near the southern trailhead, there is a little pond that beckons as a picnic spot. Then, all too soon, the trail emerges at Route 302.

Upper Coos Railroad

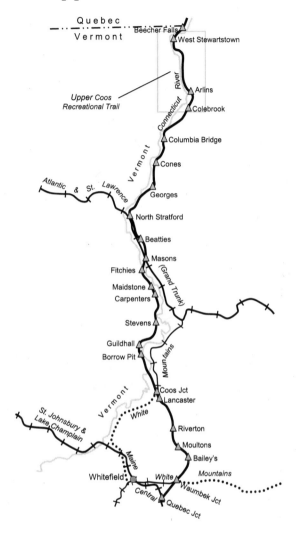

Quebec Jct. to Lime Ridge, Quebec
Built: 1888–90
Abandoned: Beecher Falls, VT–Lime Ridge, 1921; Coos Jct.–North Stratford, 1948; Quebec Jct.–Waumbek Jct., 1977.
This ambitious 108-mile railroad had fifty miles of track in New Hampshire and Vermont and another fifty-three miles in Quebec. It was built to support

lumber mills along its route and a large furniture manufacturer in Beecher Falls, VT.

Despite its length and connections with the Grand Trunk Railroad (previously and currently the St. Lawrence & Atlantic), Maine Central (previously the Portland & Ogdensburg), and the White Mountains Division of the Boston, Concord & Montreal, this line was never a busy one for either freight or passengers.

Currently the state owns the sections of the Upper Coos in New Hampshire. The Quebec Junction-to-Waumbek Junction section no longer has track. The 1.9-mile piece from Airport Road to Waumbek Junction is the first part of the Pondicherry section of the Presidential Range Rail Trail. The rails between Waumbek Junction and Coos Junction are returning to active use under the New Hampshire Central Railroad. Coos Junction to North Stratford was abandoned sixty years ago and offers no trail opportunities. The NHC uses the line from North Stratford to Columbia Bridge to serve gravel quarries and lumber mills. NHC also has a freight car repair facility in North Stratford that serves several short-line carriers. An 8.7-mile section in Colebrook and Stewartstown is now an informal rail trail with a problematic surface but excellent scenery.

N4. Upper Coos Recreational Trail

Railroad Bridge, West Stewartstown, to Colebrook Depot, 8.7 miles
Trail condition: Stewartstown section: ★★★ The track is still in place, but most of the ties have been covered with dirt to make an informal trail for hikers; **Colebrook section:** ★★ Track is still there, and the trail is heavily overgrown and impassible for all but the heartiest bushwacker in summer; it may be usable by skiers and snowmobilers in winter with a heavy snow pack.
Scenery: ★★★★★ Views of the upper Connecticut River, farms on the floodplain, and surrounding hills.
Permitted uses: Non-motorized travel year-round; snowmobiles, ATVs, and motorized trail bikes in winter only when snow-covered. Because of the rails and rough surface, hiking is the only practical way of using the trail in summer.
Right of way owned by: State of New Hampshire.
Maintained by: Trails Bureau and Colebrook Ski Bees snowmobile club.

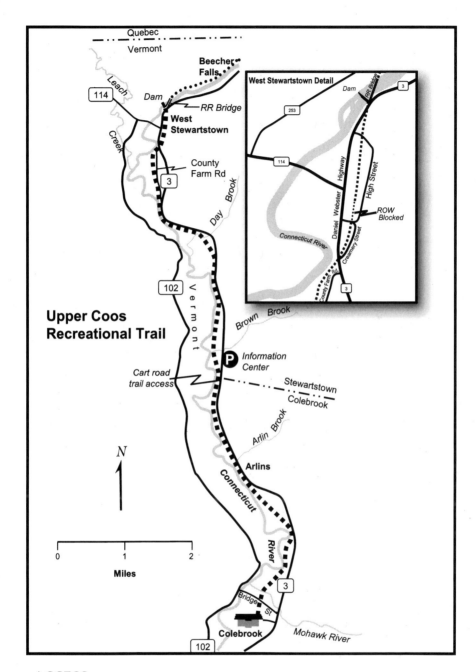

ACCESS

Despite its close proximity to Route 3, there are few good trail accesses along the way. There is plenty of street parking at West Stewartstown on the north

Paddlers enjoy the Connecticut River south of the highway bridge.

end and in Colebrook on the south end. There is also excellent parking in the center of the trail at a rest area and information center just north of the Stewartstown-Colebrook border on Route 3. It is also possible to reach the trail from cart roads off of County Farm Road and off of Route 3 just south of the information center.

DESCRIPTION

This trail goes by the Connecticut River at its scenic best. Hills and mountains surround fertile Connecticut Valley farms, and the river is clear and free-flowing. The trail surface is problematic, however, with track still in place and fast-growing weeds. With removal of the track and application of a hardpack surface, this could be one of the state's finest rail trails. Sale of the rails for scrap steel would help pay for the upgrade.

For now, this is primarily a trail for walking and winter activity. I tried to use my mountain bike and got stopped dead by an occasional exposed railroad tie. The further south I got, the more overgrown the trail became. Perhaps the best approach is to start in West Stewartstown and walk down to the cart road access at the town border near the information center.

The railroad bridge in West Stewartstown is just upstream of a small dam. By crossing the bridge, it may be possible to extend an outing to Beecher Falls on the Vermont side of the river, but I did not explore there. Below the dam, the river funnels through some rapids that canoeists usually avoid by putting in at the Route 114 bridge.

Going south from the railroad bridge, the trail parallels the Daniel Webster Highway in West Stewartstown and crosses High Street twice. Near the second High Street crossing, the right of way is blocked by weed growth and items stored by an abutter. Until the trail is properly developed, you can take one of the alleys out to the highway. Proceed a couple of blocks south to High Street and use it to return to the trail. You soon cross under a Route 3 overpass near Creamery Street, then you come to the county farm area. Views of the river, farm fields, and hills start showing the scenery potential of this path.

The trail surface is very unusual as you pass by the Coos County Farm on County Farm Road. Spaces between railroad ties have been filled with dirt, so the path is reasonably smooth for walking and tempting for bicycling. However, fast-growing vegetation seeks to reclaim the railroad bed and must be cut back frequently.

The trail features pastoral scenes like this one of a cornfield and cows.

Looking south from the cart road near the town line. Although heavily overgrown in August of 2007, this growth could easily be cut back to open the trail.

Proceeding southward, there are frequent views of farm fields, hills, and cows. The proximity to Route 3 is never a problem; there was only one spot where I got a direct view of cars.

Perhaps there is less cutting back of the growth near Colebrook. In any case, the bushwacking got progressively more intense as I went south. Also, the railroad ties became more conspicuous. Riding a bicycle was out of the question. The trail finally got so overgrown that I gave up at the cart road access near the information center, just north of the Colebrook town line.

The next place I was able to see the trail was from Bridge Street, about a third of a mile north of the depot in Colebrook. Again, it was heavily overgrown in both directions. The end of the trail appears to be the Colebrook depot, located off Colby Street.

Helpful Organizations

THE following organizations provide valuable information and resources for planning, construction, and maintenance of New Hampshire's rail trails. In addition to these listings, local historical societies can provide excellent background on the railroads, and town conservation commissions usually have the latest information on trail plans and status.

National & Statewide Agencies

Bike/Walk Alliance of NH
163 Manchester Street, Suite C
Concord, NH 03301
603-898-9926
www.bwanh.org
Lobbying group for bicycle and
  pedestrian paths

East Coast Greenway Alliance
27 North Road
Wakefield, RI 02879
401-789-4625
www.greenway.org
Consortium of groups working to
  make a trail along the entire east
  coast, including on or near the
  Eastern RR right of way in New
  Hampshire

Granite State Wheelmen
215 South Broadway
Salem, NH 03079-3309
www.granitestatewheelmen.org
Organizes both on-road and off-road
  bicycle rides

National Park Service Rivers & Trails Program
54 Elm Street
Woodstock, VT 05091
802-457-3368
www.nps.gov/rtca
Provides technical & grant
  writing support to trail groups;
  knowledgeable about rail trails

New England Mountain Bike Association
P.O. Box 2221
Acton, MA 01720
800-57-NEMBA
www.nemba.org
Organizes mountain bike rides and

trail work with multiple chapters in NE states

New Hampshire Bureau of Trails
172 Pembroke Road
Concord, NH 03301
603-271-3254
www.nhtrails.org
Manages state-owned trails

NH Bike/Ped Coordinator
7 Hazen Drive
Concord, NH 03301
603-271-1668
www.nh.gov/dot/nhbikeped
Coordinates efforts of other state agencies to insure bicycle and pedestrian ways are considered in planning

Northeast Greenway Solutions
Craig Della Penna
P.O. Box 60211
Florence, MA 01062
413-575-2277
www.greenwaysolutions.org
Produces a free monthly email newsletter with the latest rail trail developments in New England

Rails-to-Trails Conservancy
1100 17th Street NW, 10th Floor
Washington, DC 20036
202-331-9696
www.railtrails.org
Provides general information on rail trails; national lobbying group for federal funding

Local Organizations

Andover Snowmobile Club
P.O. Box 332
Andover, NH 03216
603-934-3327
www.andoversnowmobileclub.com
Snowmobile club for the Northern Rail Trail in Andover

Asquamchumauke Valley Snowmobile Club
426 Tarleton Road
Warren, NH 03279
603-764-5222
www.avscnh.org
Snowmobile club for the Warren Recreational Trail

Belmont BRATT
603-528-4345
www.belmontnh.org/bds_bratt.asp
Volunteer group developing the Belmont section of the Winnipesaukee Trail

Cotton Valley Rail Trail Club
www.cottonvalley.org
Runs railroad section cars & maintains the Cotton Valley Trail

Derry Rail Trail Alliance
5 Wilson Avenue
Derry, NH 03038
603-537-1120
www.derryrailtrail.org
Volunteer group improving the portion of the Manchester & Lawrence right of way in Derry

Friends of Pondicherry
515 Bailey Street
Jefferson, NH 03583
Planning and maintenance group for the Presidential Range Rail Trail

Friends of the Northern Rail Trail–Grafton County
Box 206
Enfield, NH 03748
www.northernrailtrail.org
Group that built and now maintains the Northern Rail Trail from Lebanon through Grafton

Friends of the Northern Rail Trail–Merrimack County

P.O. Box 154
Andover, NH 03216
www.fnrt.org
Group building and upgrading the four-season Northern Rail Trail in Merrimack County

Hands Across the Merrimack

300 River Road, Office Suite 2
Manchester, NH 03104
Activist group behind the renovation of the railroad bridge over the Merrimack River in Manchester as a pedestrian bridge

Hooper Hill Hoppers Snowmobile Club

P.O. Box 142
Walpole, NH 03608
Snowmobile club extending the Cheshire North Trail in Walpole

Keene Sno-Riders

P.O. Box 1511
Keene, NH 03431
603-352-8237
www.KeeneSnoRiders.com
Snowmobile club for the Ashuelot and Cheshire North Trails

Laconia Trails with Rails Exploratory Committee

Greater Laconia/Weirs Beach
Chamber of Commerce
393 South Main Street
Laconia, NH 03246
603-524-5531
www.wowtrail.org
Group developing the Winnisquam-Opechee-Winnipesaukee (WOW) section of the Winnipesaukee Trail

Lakes Region Snowmobile Club

P.O. Box 6008
Franklin NH 03235-6008
603-496-5811
www.lakesregionsnowmobileclub.com
Snowmobile club for the Northern Rail Trail in Franklin

Littleton Offroad Riders

P.O. Box 281
Littleton, NH 03561
www.littletonareachamber.com/activities.php
Multi-user trail group for the Ammonoosuc Recreational Trail

Meredith Rail Trail Committee

83 Windsong Place
Meredith, NH 03253
603-279-5084
www.MeredithRailTrail.org
Group developing the Meredith section of the Winnipesaukee Trail

Monadnock Sno-Moles

P.O. Box 265
Rindge, NH 03461-0265
www.snomoles.org
Snowmobile club for the Cheshire South and Monadnock Recreational Trails

New Common Pathway Committee

www.townofpeterborough.com
Town committee responsible for planning and constructing trails in Peterborough

Pathways for Keene

www.tlaorg.org/pathways/
Promotes trails in Keene and helps maintain the Cheshire, Ashuelot, and Fort Hill Recreational Trails

Presidential Range Riders

P.O. Box 141
Gorham, NH 03581
Snowmobile club for the eastern part of the Presidential Range Rail Trail

Queen City Trail Alliance

www.queencitytrails.org
Volunteer group building the trail
on the Manchester portion of the
Manchester & Lawrence rail line

Shugah Valley Sno Riders

P.O. Box 944
Claremont, NH 03743
www.svsrclub.org
Snowmobile club for the Sugar River
Rail Trail

Southern NH Snow Slickers

73 Tower Hill Road
Candia, NH 03034
www.snowslickers.org
Snowmobile club for the Portsmouth
Branch Trail

Swanzey Bike Path Committee

P.O. Box 10009,
Swanzey, NH 03446
603-352-7411
Will pave part of the Ashuelot
Recreational Trail in Swanzey

Townline Trail Dusters

P.O. Box 3031
Boscawen, NH 03303
www.townlinetraildusters.com
Snowmobile club for the Boscawen
section of the Northern Rail Trail

Trails Rails Action Committee (TRAC)

P. O. Box 111
Wakefield, NH 03872
Group planning a multi-use trail for
the entire Wolfeboro Railroad right
of way

Tri County OHRV

P.O. Box 950
Hillsboro, NH 03244-0950
OHRV club for the Hillsboro
Recreational Trail

Twin State Trailbusters

P.O. Box 858
Lebanon, NH 03766
Snowmobile club for the Northern Rail
Trail in Lebanon and Enfield

Westmoreland Sno-Belters

P.O. Box 8
Westmoreland, NH 03467
Snowmobile club for the Cheshire
North Trail

Whitefield Sno-Kings

P.O. Box 64
Whitefield, NH 03598
www.snokings.com
Snowmobile club for the Presidential
Range Rail Trail, Pondicherry Section

Winchester Trail Riders

P.O. Box 225
Winchester, NH 03470
603-239-6853
www.winchestertrailriders.org
Snowmobile club for the Ashuelot
Recreational Trail

Windham Rail Trail Alliance

P.O. Box 4317
Windham, NH 03087
603-434-0806
www.windhamrailtrail.org
Group that built the Windham Rail
Trail and is now renovating the depot

Winnipesaukee River Trail Association

P.O. Box 464
Franklin, NH 03235
www.lakesregion.org/groups/winni_
river.html
Group that built and maintains the
Winnipesaukee River Trail and
Trestle View Park

Additional Resources

MOST OF the information for this book came from personal scouts, talking to trail experts, and Robert M. Lindsell's *The Rail Lines of Northern New England*. Organizations listed in the previous chapter are excellent sources of information. In addition, there are a few sources of general information listed here that you should find particularly helpful.

Trail Information

NHRailTrails.org is a web site for this book maintained by the author. It lists errata and updates trail developments since publication of the book. If you find errors or omissions in the book or have suggestions for changes, please send them to Charles@NHRailTrails.org for posting on this web site.

The official web site for the New Hampshire Bureau of Trails is NHTrails.org. This site lists state-owned rail trails and discusses the Trails Bureau role, upcoming meetings, grant activity, and other news about state trails. The Recreational Rail Trails page lists permitted uses on each trail the bureau manages.

BWANH.org is the web site of the Bike/Walk Alliance of New Hampshire. It is a good source for information about general issues regarding trails in the state.

Two web sites should keep you informed about the ongoing controversy concerning use of state-owned rail trails in the winter by off-highway recreational vehicles. NHOHVA.org is the web site of the New Hampshire Off Highway Vehicle Association. It represents the viewpoint of ATV and motorized trail bike users concerning state trails. ATVWatch.org, maintained by the ATV Watch organization, is fervently opposed to ATV use.

Maps

DeLorme's *New Hampshire Atlas & Gazetteer* (Yarmouth, ME: DeLorme), a large-format paperback book of detailed road maps is indispensable in finding one's way around New Hampshire. It is available everywhere,in drug stores, book stores, department stores, even wholesale clubs. The *New Hampshire Atlas* will give you a clear context for how the maps in this book relate to the road system.

Many of our railroads disappeared so long ago that it is hard to find out where their rights of way went. The *Historic USGS Maps of New England* (http://docs.unh.edu/digital.htm, Durham, NH: University of New Hampshire Library) are a complete set of old-time United States Geological Survey topographic maps of New Hampshire from the early- to mid-twentieth century. They show the railroads and their surroundings when they were in operation.

If you want to see an aerial view of New Hampshire trails from NASA satellite photos, *Google Earth* lets you get good close-ups. Moreover, it has an excellent, up-to-date road layer. *Google Earth* is available on line at http://earth.google.com. You have to download software to your personal computer to access the data over the Internet. I used *Google Earth* as a source to check road names and locations and to draw some of the detail maps.

Street Atlas USA, also from DeLorme, is a software program that comes as CD-ROMs and is updated each year. It can help you understand detailed road layouts for areas that are not covered in *Google Earth* or the *New Hampshire Atlas*.

TOPO! Northeastern USA (Evergreen, CO: National Geographic Society, 2003) is another software program in CD-ROM format. It gives you topographic maps in five levels of successively higher resolution. The presentation is seamless, meaning you don't have to worry about quadrangle boundaries, as you do with the paper USGS topographic maps.

Mike Walker's *Comprehensive Railroad Atlas of North America: New England & Maritime Canada* (Kent, United Kingdom: SPV, 1999) shows where all the New Hampshire railroads went and labels all of their stations. It serves as a cross-check to the information on antique topographic maps and in *The Rail Lines of Northern New England*. Beware that railroad stations often changed over time, so these sources may not always agree on the existence or names of stations.

Railroad History

Robert M. Lindsell's *The Rail Lines of Northern New England* (Pepperell, MA: Branch Line Press, 2000) is an incredibly valuable book with four- to five-page historical summaries for each of New Hampshire's railroads. I was so impressed that it led me to publish *New Hampshire Rail Trails* with Branch Line Press.

Logging Railroads of the White Mountains by C. Francis Belcher (Boston, MA: Appalachian Mountain Club, 1980) is a classic. It provides a good overview of the logging railroads used by the timber barons at the end of the nineteenth century to clear-cut the vast forests of the White Mountains.

For more detailed histories of the logging railroads, you should obtain the following books by Bill Gove (all from Bondcliff Books in Littleton, NH). *J. E. Henry's Logging Railroads* (1998) describes the most notorious of all the lumber barons, J. E. Henry, and the two railroads he built: Zealand Valley and East Branch & Lincoln. After you admire the locomotive and log truck at Loon Mountain, you might want to pick up this book to get the whole story. *Logging Railroads of the Saco River Valley* (2001) outlines the history of several timber railroads: Sawyer River, Bartlett & Albany, Saco Valley, and Conway Company. The Sawyer River right of way still exists as road and trail, as described in *Rail-Trails New England* (Berkeley, CA: Wilderness Press, 2007). *Logging Railroads Along the Pemigewasset River* (2006) describes the Pemigewasset Valley, Gordon Pond, Woodstock & Thornton Gore, Beebe River, and W. D. Veazey Railroads.

There are two wonderful collections of historical New England railroad pictures, books, maps, and memorabilia. The Walker Collection, which was assembled by Lawrence Breed Walker after he developed polio, resides at the Beverly Historical Society and Museum, 117 Cabot Street, Beverly, MA (www.walkertrans.org). This collection, which has continued to grow since the museum acquired it, includes many photographs of the railroads of New Hampshire while they were still operating. The collection of the Boston & Maine Railroad Historical Society (www.trainweb.org/bmrrhs), including all issues of its *B&M Bulletin*, is currently housed in the University of Massachusetts Lowell's Center for Lowell History at 40 French Street, Lowell, MA. Call 978-454-3600 or write to B&MRRHS, P.O. Box 469, Derry, NH 03038-0469 for information.

Index

About the Author

CHARLES F. MARTIN was trained in mathematics, with a bachelor's degree from Harvard and Ph.D. from the University of California, Berkeley. In his professional life, he is an operations research analyst with a career devoted to decision support software. He is currently Director of Product Management for Valogix LLC, an inventory optimization software firm.

In his personal life, Charles has always enjoyed getting into the great outdoors and exploring beautiful new places. An expert whitewater paddler, his first book was *Sierra Whitewater: A Paddler's Guide to Rivers in California's Sierra Nevada* (now out of print). Charles has been active in the rails-to-trails movement since 2002, when he started working with the Friends of the Bruce Freeman Rail Trail in Concord, MA. Since moving to New Hampshire in 2005, he has been an active member of the Friends of the Northern Rail Trail in Merrimack County. He is on the board and is currently treasurer of this group, which is developing the thirty-four-mile Merrimack County stretch of the Northern Rail Trail as a four-season trail. This book is part of Charles's expanded effort to encourage improvement of rail trails across the state and to spread appreciation for them.

You may email the author at Charles@NHRailTrails.org.

The author on the Northern Rail Trail (Amy Martin Webster)